The New Hawsepipe

A Comprehensive Guide
to Merchant Marine Licensing and Documentation

The New Hawsepipe

A Comprehensive Guide
to Merchant Marine Licensing and Documentation

By Leonard Lambert

P.O. Box 456
Centreville, Maryland 21617

Library of Congress Cataloging-in-Publication Data
Lambert, Leonard, 1972-
   The New Hawsepipe : a comprehensive guide to merchant marine licensing
and documentation / by Leonard Lambert.
      p. cm.
   Includes index.
   ISBN 978-0-87033-587-7
1. Merchant marine--Vocational guidance--United States. 2. Merchant marine--United States--Examinations, questions, etc. 3. Merchant marine--United States--Officers. 4. Merchant mariners--United States--Education. I. Title. II. Title: Comprehensive guide to merchant marine licensing and documentation.

   VK160.L36 2007
   387.5023'73--dc22

   2007008729

"Passport Renewal Available at No Charge" by Ken Walsh, reprinted from *Master Mates and Pilots Weekly* Newsletter

Designed by Stacie Tingen

Manufactured in the United States of America
First Edition; first printing, 2007

These instructions apply to license applicants who are NOT participating in a formal training program of instruction such as presented at a maritime academy. These instructions apply to mariners who are "coming through the hawsepipe."

National Maritime Center Policy Letter [01-02], Applicability Section

Acknowledgments

I would like to thank Lisa Albers, who contributed immensely to this book. She is the former editor of Fisherman's News and current editor with Moss Adams in Seattle. Without her knowledge and creativity of the English language and belief in the subject matter, I would not have been able to publish the book.

I would also like to thank BMC Jennifer Hogge from the United States Coast Guard for her expertise in the subject matter and the pursuit of a better, safer, more knowledgeable merchant mariner.

Table of Contents

Introduction
How to Use This Book

This book is a reference guide for receiving any U.S. Coast Guard (USCG) deck license or Merchant Mariner's Document (MMD). Its purpose is to outline every step in the process, from just starting out as a new mariner to achieving the rank of captain. It will explain the history of the industry and why we are where we are today. It will pave a realistic path from the beginning until the end. Keep this book with you while you climb through the new hawsepipe to your new license or MMD.

Whether you are just getting started in the industry or have more time on the deck of a ship than in your own living room, you must negotiate the rules governing maritime licensing. Trying to figure out which mix of sea time, specialized training and USCG testing will allow you to make a better living as an able-bodied seaman (AB), mate, or captain can be frustrating. Indeed, most career mariners become seagoing encyclopedias to ensure they keep up with changes and possess the adequate endorsements to get or keep the job they want.

Keeping up with licensing requirements will be a full-time job in your maritime career, whether you like it or not. The aim of this book is to arm you with the resources for advancing your career efficiently. The tasks laid out in this book are not easy, and the license or MMD you receive will be a true accomplishment.

Realize that USCG licenses and MMDs are the rewards of playing a game. In this game, you need to fulfill separate tasks. Some are as easy as knowing your own name and proving you are able to work in the United States. Others are as difficult as completing seventy-eight practical assessments you have never done before, and having them signed by a senior officer who doesn't really know who you are.

When you are on a ship, the grandeur of being an officer or captain is always strong. That is the top of the ladder. Captains are some of the highest-paid officers and hold the ultimate responsibility. Many mariners want to advance their careers. The reality is many mariners start the process, some complete it, and few actually receive their licenses. To be one of those who finish the program and receive the license or MMD is an absolute victory, and the benefits, in this game, outweigh the costs. When I sailed as an AB for one year to get the sea time I needed to apply for my unlimited third mate's license, I received $43,000 for the work. The following year that I received my license and sailed six months as a third mate I made $85,000, almost double my income in half the time. What other profession allows you to double your income in one year and work less time doing it? Believe me, it is worth it and it is obtainable.

The key to making your way up the hawsepipe is setting small goals in realistic time frames. Information given in this book will reference certain time periods throughout the licensing process and suggest how best to use them. For example, the USCG has an evaluation process for your license or MMD application. This process can take anywhere from two weeks to six months, depending on the workload at the Coast Guard. During that time, students can be taking courses that do not pertain to the license, but are additional classes needed for employment on certain vessels; or the time could be spent studying for the USCG examination. When the application approval arrives from the USCG, the exam can be taken immediately. Always remember to use time to your advantage.

The confidence of knowledge is the utmost reward. Many a frustrated mariner has left the Coast Guard Regional Exam Center (REC) more confused than when they entered. Do not be afraid to ask anything and everything. Talk to maritime schools, the Coast Guard, fellow shipmates (especially the new hawsepipers), or contact me via www.thenewhawsepipe.com Web site.

Use any and all means to obtain the information you need. The responsibility falls solely upon you to figure out what it is you need to do, and there is a lot to do. Every ship has a number of unlicensed crew wanting to upgrade to an officer's license, be the one who makes it.

Many tools are out there and this book will help you use them to get what you want.

Chapter One
Motivation

Of all the hurdles you have to overcome in obtaining a license, the most important, by far, is mustering the motivation to complete the task.

Imagine this: Your boss approaches you one day while you are working on some menial project, but thinking about something else, and he says, "My! What a great job you've been doing! You know, you are just the kind of person we need to run our operation. I'll tell you what: Why don't you take the rest of the year off, paid and with benefits, of course, and get all the necessary qualifications and training you need to run the show. In fact, while you are finding out what you need, we would be more than happy to assist you with any questions that you might have. You'll have the company and the U.S. government at your fingertips to take care of any problem as fast as possible. Oh, and don't forget, as soon as you get done jumping through all these hoops for us, you can start at your new job immediately with a pay raise and better perks!"

This is about the time the phone rings on the bulkhead with the same familiar voice that has been waking you up for the last three months saying, "Next watch." Fantasize all you want, but the boss is never going to give you such an invitation.

We live in a world in which the hierarchy is written: crew, ship, cargo. But the harsh reality is that sometimes the true order of business is cargo, ship, crew. A sailor's job is to get things from point A to point B safely and efficiently, and there is little time for much else. Sailors are travelers of the land and sea, investigating all corners of the world to find solutions to major world problems like, "Where can I get a beer in this place?" or, "Which currency is my wallet stuffed with now?"

The most important chapter in this book is also one of the shortest. Its message can be summed up in one sentence: No one cares if you get your license but you. This is a harsh truth, but a necessary one. Too many barriers are before you: lack of knowledge (the people you are asking don't really know), incompetence (they think they know, but they don't), indifference (they know, but don't care whether you know), and, the worst, attitude (they know, but don't want you to know because you are not "one of them"). Motivate yourself to understand what is needed to complete the job. In the end, it will be your name and your name alone stamped on the license. After all the hard work to obtain it, this reward will be well deserved. Each task detailed in this book requires motivation. You should expect to spend free time reading manuals and practicing assessments instead of watching a movie or enjoying a meal out. It also means approaching higher-ranking members of the crew and soliciting their help during their workday or time off.

The single greatest test of your motivation will be how well you convince those in positions of authority to help you through the licensing process. Ideally, an initiative to learn from the student will be met with equal initiative from the teacher to teach, but this is not always the case. For example, an unlicensed crewmember is trying to get the practical assessments signed off onboard ship by a second officer or higher. This is a classic example of the student teaching the teacher. To advance through the hawsepipe, you have to show them what you need. Unlike in the military, there is no formal training process on which to draw. It takes motivation as an unlicensed crewmember to learn what is needed for this task, present your needs and your case to your superiors, and carry out the task to the satisfaction of your superiors, obtaining their signature of approval, which is the ultimate goal.

The motivation to learn, the motivation to be confident in what you have learned, and the motivation to present what you have learned to a superior officer is a process every student needs to undergo. This is mandatory for completing the tasks for a license with your superior officers, maritime instructors, USCG personnel, and fellow shipmates. It is your responsibility to read, understand, and fulfill all requirements for the license or document for which you are applying.

Motivation is cultivated with realistic goals. The tasks must be set according to the mariner's lifestyle. Do not think that getting your MMD or license will happen overnight or even in a year or two. This is where most mariners get frustrated and quit. There is no instant gratification in this process. A mariner might have a family, like to travel, or have hefty bills. The point is not to rule out the possibility of achieving your goal, but set it realistically. It might take you five years to complete the training, taking classes when convenient and affordable, getting sea time when necessary, and so on. As long as the goals have been set to a five-year plan, you should be able to obtain a license. When I made the decision to upgrade my license, I sacrificed one year to school. I shed all my financial responsibilities, lived like a hermit, ate, slept, and drank this program. I went to any school in the country that had the classes I needed, and applied to any financial aid program that would help me. I sacrificed all my free time onboard ships to shadow the chief and second mates, so they would sign my assessments. It took me one full year to get my license. Maybe my example is an extreme case, but no matter how long it takes, it can be done. Plan to work on it without going nuts or alienating your family. A realistic time frame is to get off a ship, enjoy some time with the family on a planned vacation, and take no more than two classes while you are off. This way, you can balance your time off, fulfilling your family and career goals. While in those classes, look down the road to the next time you will be on vacation and schedule the next set of classes right then. When you get back on a ship, get a chunk of the practical assessments signed relating to the subject matter of the upcoming classes. This way, when you get off the ship again, you will be knowledgeable in those subjects and the classes will not be as difficult. Repeat this process until you are done.

Someone once said that something of value usually takes a sacrifice to get it. That is why it is of value. This program is just that. It takes planning, sacrifice, and communication between your family and friends, but it is worth it.

Most importantly, this will not work unless your *whole* family is behind you. Motivation is key to keeping your eye on the prize and maintaining your family's understanding of what you are doing. Make sure you communicate all the time. After a class, show them the certificates, talk about what kind of job you will be doing, and never over-promise anything. Any disappointment will lead to a bigger burden of completion, so plan, plan, plan!

When I stepped onto my first ship as an AB, I met with the captain in the huge office he had, knowing full well that he was the highest-paid person on this ship (along with the Chief Engineer). I realized that throughout the trip, the captain did relatively little outside of his office. He seemed to sit around taking phone calls, doing paperwork, and typing on the computer. As I was outside tearing apart the anchor windless, I thought to myself, I want to be the captain—what a job! The point is, most people think that way. Why wouldn't you want to sit around all day and make a lot more money?

However, as I came to realize, the ultimate responsibility of the vessel, cargo, and crew constantly weighs on the captain's shoulders. If anything goes wrong onboard, the chain of responsibility goes straight up to the captain. I also learned they are not always in the office behind the computer. Sometimes they go to the radio room or to the gym (if you have one). Seriously, it is the captain who will face the ultimate consequences if anything happens. My point is, not everyone is cut out for that kind of job and responsibility. Some shy away. Some just don't need it in their lives and are happy where they are. Some don't want to enter the competition for a captain's job.

The ultimate goal is contentment. To be happy with your job as much as possible. You're going to spend a lot of time at it, so you need to like it, at least a little bit. This means making decisions based on your quality of life. Some folks are happy being an AB or Ordinary Seaman (OS) and wouldn't have it any other way. Leave the officer stuff to the officers and leave the AB stuff to the ABs. A ship works well when everyone knows his or her place in the chain of command and nobody is stepping on anyone, slacking off, or not towing the line. If you're happy where you are, stay there. Ships need good ABs, good OSs, and so on. Do not plunge into the hawsepipe unless you are serious about finishing it.

I was planning on getting into the remodeling business for homes that had been rundown—buy them, fix them up, and then sell them for profit. I knew a number of people that made a great living doing it, and I wanted to get in. I picked up a book about it—Robert Irwin's *Find It, Buy it, Fix It*. Irwin had been doing that kind of work for thirty years. His first chapter said you must have three things to be successful and enjoy this type of work: 1) The time to do it. If you struggle with free time to engage in these projects, you will prolong it to the extent of no longer being profitable. 2) The money to do it. If you cannot borrow or use liquid cash for securing properties, it will be very difficult to obtain those great deals that could come along at any time. 3) Most important of all is the commitment to the project. If you do *not* like living in an unfinished kitchen, having the water off for weeks, toilets that do not work and everyday problems that will constantly change, this is *not* the path for you. You will become so frustrated that you will begin to hate the house, hate the job, and eventually sell it for a loss just to get out of doing it. To prevent this, the best decision is not to even get started.

The rest of the book made a convincing case that you could make a good living at remodeling homes and fixing them up for a profit. But that first chapter kept resonating in my mind. Would I be happy coming home from a four-month job on a ship, to be met with sawdust everywhere, unfinished kitchens and bathrooms? How would I continue my plan to upgrade my license if I was burdened with working on a house?

Heeding my gut feeling, I decided not to pursue this venture. Instead, I focused on what I needed to do to get my license. As I said before, it took me one year to complete all the classes, Coast Guard tests, and practical assessments. Ask yourself that same question—Do I really want to do this? I cannot emphasize enough that you need to plan all the tasks so you can complete them. From gaining sea time, to the license and MMD application process, testing, assessments, classes, time with family, time off, finances—all this needs to be thought out. As in my case with the houses, think hard about whether you want to make the commitment. You might enjoy where you are, and that is perfectly fine. If you're happy, stay there. Go all the way or don't go at all.

After I figured out that I did not want to remodel houses and was going for the license, I was able to buy a brand new, half million dollar, 3,000 square foot home on a half acre from the money I earned as an officer.

I know of only a few people who have completed the program from AB to mate and are sailing on their licenses. One is a friend with whom I was in the Coast Guard. He sails for the International Organization of Masters, Mates and Pilots (IOMM&P). When he started, his plan was a two-year plan, sacrificing as much money and time as he could. His motivation was tested a number of times, and he ended up almost quitting near the end because it got too frustrating for him. He told me the hardest thing he did was push through the last sections of his classes and assessments, living in a one-room shack, trying to pay for classes and studying, while the maritime schools jerked him around with schedules and prices for classes. His motivation is a reaffirmation of what I am talking about. Happily, he has paid all his debt and is making great money in a job he really likes.

Assume this will happen to you. At any given time, a class will be too hard, you won't have filled out a form you needed, schools and companies will not cooperate with your schedule, you will have unforeseen bills, or lack extra money. All these things take sacrifice, motivation, and focus to overcome.

I have another friend who is just starting as an AB at a coastal tanker company. He got the job not only because of the money and the routes, but, more importantly, because they had a program for hawsepipers. This kind of forethought is crucial. When you make the choice to advance, every decision you make should be for that purpose until the goal is met. When I started, I realized I needed seven more months of sea time. Now, I could have gotten it anywhere, providing the ship was the correct tonnage. But I didn't really care what the job or the money really was; I was concerned about the courses I needed to take and whether the company or union would provide them for me.

I called around and talked to lots of different unions and companies. I settled on Seafarers International Union (SIU) based solely on the schooling they provided. I worked as an AB for nine months to get the rest of my sea time. On my off time I went to the union school in Piney Point, Maryland, to get a lot of my training. It was a very fair trade. I completed half of all my classes there and it got me off to a good start.

Merchant mariners trying to obtain licenses and MMDs from the Coast Guard often stare at the mountain of new information and requirements needed to complete the task. But what is most important is to keep the flame of motivation alive at all times and your license is totally obtainable. You show the motivation, the Coast Guard will show you your license. Now, go get it.

Chapter Two
The Maritime Regulatory System

In any game, the key to a winning strategy begins with knowing the rules. It also helps to understand the intentions of the rule makers. The laws governing maritime licensing are shaped in reaction to human failure and accidents at sea. Maritime history is punctuated by legendary disasters—the *Titanic, Torrey Canyon, Valdez,* and *Arctic Rose* are just a few well-known examples. These famous accidents serve as reminders that ships and humans are not invincible. People die, ships sink, environments are ruined, and money and cargo lost. Each historic disaster provided a case study from which the rules were tightened to avoid similar calamity. Licensing requirements are designed to prevent repeat disasters. Although navigating the web of rules and regulations can seem daunting, it is hard to fault regulators for making our profession safer. Too bad safer isn't simpler.

The global shipping industry is one of the largest businesses in the world, and shipping is one of the oldest professions. Because so many countries rely on maritime transportation, there is a potential for a great deal of confusion, contradiction, and regulatory gap, or overlap.

Fortunately for the mariner, maritime regulations have been globally standardized. Take the example of McDonald's. Why do all the Big Macs in the world taste the same? It does not matter what country you are visiting, McDonald's food tastes like McDonald's. Customers rely on that, and McDonald's does a pretty good job of standardizing its operations, recipes, and service throughout the world. The question is, how? The answer is: regulations. McDonald's ensures that every restaurant adheres to the regulations of the central corporation.

The shipping industry is becoming the same, although it is apparent by the training and treatment of the mariners that some countries and companies clearly are not party to these regulations. Because so many different countries are involved, there is the potential to have the business run many different ways. There is a global chain of command, and merchant mariners are basically employees of this global business and answerable to these regulations. The following entities are charged with governing global maritime business to the parties that are actively involved with these standardized regulations.

► The International Maritime Organization (IMO). The United Nations (UN) established the IMO at the Geneva Convention in 1948. Its sole purpose is to regulate global shipping and ensure countries adhere to the safety and environmental protection standards put forth by the UN. The United States became party to the IMO in 1991 and was an active member in forming the Standards in Training and Certification of Watchkeeping (STCW). Visit the IMO Web site for more information on its history and regulations at: www.imo.org.

► Federal Government. The regulations set forth by the IMO are ratified into general and permanent rules by the executive departments and agencies of the federal government in the form of the *Code of Federal Regulations* (CFR) and *United States Code* (USC). The CFR and USC govern our shipping industry. Learning the basics of these codes is imperative for shipping and licensing by mariners. The CFR is available online at: www. gpoaccess.gov/cfr/index.html, and the USC is listed at the U.S. House of Representatives' Web site at: www.uscode.house. gov/usc.htm

► National Maritime Center. The National Maritime Center is the field branch of the USCG. Its purpose is to translate the CFR and USC into plain English in the form of Policy Letters and National Vessel Inspection Circulars (NVIC). These letters are distributed to the USCG branches for enforcement and are labeled "Policy and Guidance." The National Maritime Center Web site address is: www.uscg.mil/hq/g-m/nmc/web/index. htm.

► U.S. Coast Guard. This is the government body with which the merchant mariner most often associates. The enforcement of STCW and all the merchant mariner regulations lie with the USCG. Mariners seeking licenses will become familiar with the RECs, found throughout the country. Mariners must submit documents and take exams at RECs, and these offices issue licenses and MMDs. I will cover the RECs in more detail in the next chapter.

Now that the players have been briefly described, here is the chain of events that led to the modern shipping industry and STCW 95.

The IMO had set safety standards to which signatory countries had to adhere. This was the STCW, and these standards were put into practice in 1978, hence STCW 78.

After the United States became party to the IMO and STCW 78, a growing concern developed. Countries, including the United States, questioned whether the IMO was really enforcing the training standards in every country party to the STCW. The training itself came under scrutiny as marine accidents continued to occur, and the innovation and technology aboard ships was not taken into consideration by STCW 78.

In December of 1992, the United States proposed a formal review of STCW 78 after the grounding of the M/V *Aegean Sea* off the coast of Spain. The U.S. proposed that the regulations regarding the human element in marine shipping, specifically crew training and fitness, be intensified. Other delegates to the IMO agreed that the time had come to revise STCW 78.

Only a month later, in January 1993, the Merchant Vessel *Braer* grounded off the Shetland Islands. The IMO was pressured to take immediate action on the STCW.

A consulting group was formed to review these marine incidents. The group submitted a letter to the IMO suggesting improvements to training and shipboard practices to prevent additional groundings and accidents.

The consulting group also offered specific amendments to the STCW in the form of a draft, so the problems and proposed solutions had been identified. The IMO assigned a subcommittee to formally review the consulting group's drafts to modify and amend the STCW 78. This was to be done by 1996.

The following May, the Secretary General of the IMO stated that the 1996 deadline for revisions was too distant and moved the deadline to July 1995. During the next two years, the IMO subcommittee worked to ratify issues to improve training, fitness and certification of mariners, port control, communication, and information and allow mutual oversight and consistency in the application of all standards. This meant the IMO would be a better global watchdog of STCW for all parties involved.

Like all legal and political amendments, the amendment of STCW did not happen overnight. Public opinion questionnaires were sent out, soliciting information, and many revisions were made. Finally, the package was approved, and STCW was officially amended. The name became *STCW 1978, as amended in 1995.*

For U.S. merchant mariners, it became STCW 95. The new rules were put into effect February 1, 2002. This meant that any mariner applying for an original license or MMD, or upgrading or renewing an existing license or MMD after February 1, 2002, would be subject to the new rules of STCW 95. The mariners who had been sailing for years on their license or MMD were grandfathered in and were required to take only one or two classes to keep current.

Many mariners lost their MMDs and licenses for failure to satisfy the new standards. For example, the Basic Safety Training (BST) class requires a mariner to don a survival suit and get into an inflated life raft from the water. The surprise came when many seasoned mariners gave up their documents because they did not know how to swim. It sent many merchant mariners looking for other professions, preferably on land.

The actual STCW 95 book (yes, there is a book) is pretty lengthy. I will focus on the U.S. merchant marine licensing and documentation section. Along with STCW 95, I will look at the additional requirements pertaining to homeland security and federal regulations.

The basic change in STCW 95 for mariners is the standardized training and competency. All mariners fitting into the category of STCW 95 must take the same training to learn and prove shipboard skills before signing onto a vessel.

The first thing to look at is the application of the STCW 95 and which rules apply to which MMDs or licenses. The STCW 95 is simple. Any mariner (officer or unlicensed) going on a transit outside U.S. waters (two hundred nautical miles [NM] offshore or international waters) is subject to STCW 95. All your domestic voyages (inside two hundred NM from U.S. shoreline) do not need the STCW 95. For example, if you work on a harbor tug in San Francisco, you do not need STCW 95. If the company decides they want that particular tug to sail to Honolulu, Hawaii, you need to be in compliance with STCW 95.

There are other considerations regarding the range of STCW 95. If you are in Puget Sound operating a ferry boat, you do not need STCW 95. If that particular ferry needs to be taken up to

Alaska via the Inside Passage, you will never be two hundred NM offshore, but you will be in Canadian waters, which means you need the STCW 95 certificate. Here is the official definition from the Coast Guard Web site:

STCW-95 applies to all present and future mariners who wish to sail beyond the boundary lines of the United States on commercial vessels. (The "boundary lines" essentially separate the bays, harbors and other inland waters from the oceans. The U.S. exempts mariners from STCW requirements who serve on small passenger vessels inspected under subchapters T and K and other vessels of less than 200 gross tons sailing on near coastal, domestic voyages. A near coastal, domestic voyage is one that begins and ends in a U.S. port, does not touch at a foreign port or enter foreign waters, and is not more than 200 miles from shore.

Subchapters T and K, in this definition, are referring to the CFR. I will talk about the CFRs, as they play a huge role in a merchant mariner's life. Learning the CFRs is like having your teeth pulled, but they can be very helpful.

These specific CFR subchapters (T and K) are about small passenger vessels and the requirements for them—licensing, tonnage, everything. 46CFR Subchapter T deals with "Small passenger vessels (under 100 gross tons)" and Subchapter K deals with "Small Passenger Vessels Carrying More Than 150 Passengers or With Overnight Accommodations for More Than 49 Passengers."

If you work on a vessel or are trying to get certified to work on a vessel that fits into either of these categories, talk to the Coast Guard about the STCW 95. Read the definitions above carefully regarding domestic voyages, small passenger vessels, and near-coastal voyages. You might not need STCW 95 if you work on a vessel that fits the exemption descriptions above.

The STCW 95 might not apply to you, but I would still take the BST classes to cover your bases. You will find more companies and unions requiring BST, even though their vessels might not be subject to it.

To make yourself more marketable as a mariner, the STCW 95 certificate will allow you to work on vessels that require it, opening more jobs for you and the ability to make more money. Being transferable is the key. Your dream job might appear and you would not be able to take it because you do not have the STCW 95.

Chapter Three
Overview of the Merchant Marines: Sea Time and What It Means

Sea time is like the fingerprint of a merchant mariner. It outlines our experience and builds our resume. Sea time, or credit for it, can be found in most facets of the maritime industry, and sea time is what qualifies mariners for MMDs and officer's licenses.

It is the details of that sea time that is of particular interest to the USCG in placing mariners with the correct and best document or license they can get. The merchant marine industry has many different licenses and documents, from the bodies of water a mariner works in, to the kind of work the mariner does, to the size of the ship on which the mariner works. This gets very confusing, and usually the mariner just hands the USCG a bunch of papers and asks, "What can I get with this?"

This chapter will break down all the requirements of each document and license, STCW applicability, how to present proof of sea time to the Coast Guard, all credits and restrictions to sea time, and where to find the references on the USCG Web site requiring the sea time for each document or license. This way the sea time can be streamlined to fit exactly to the mariner's desired document or license and sea time is not wasted. I will quote directly from the CFR, using italics to emphasize aspects of the code that need particular attention. I would hate for you to skim past something that affects your progress through the hawsepipe.

USCG licenses and documents rely on three major things: tonnage, rank, and scope. All licenses and documents are laid out in this fashion. They also can pertain to a type of work, like Offshore Supply Vessels or Uninspected Fishing Vessels, but those too are governed by tonnage, rank, and scope.

The licensed rank category has masters and mates. Only in the scope of unlimited tonnage, or "any gross tons," are third mate, second mate, and chief mate before unlimited master. The rest are limited tonnage mates with no numbers or rankings on the license.

Tonnage is the weight class of vessel to which your sea time relates. The highest tonnage is unlimited, or any gross tons (GT), anything more than 1,600 GT/3,000 GT International Tonnage Certificate (ITC), down to 25 GT vessels. There are increments in between to cover all types of vessels on the water. Tonnage allows or restricts mariners to operate vessels by their rank. For example, a 1,600 GT master can operate as a captain on a 300 GT vessel. An unlimited third mate, even with more tonnage allowance, cannot serve as master until he obtains a master's license for that tonnage. However, that third mate can serve any mate's position because of the unlimited tonnage allowance on their mate's license. Only on vessels more than 1,600 GT (unlimited) would the third mate have to stick to the third mate billet. On the other hand, a mariner that has a 1,600 ton master's license can sail any mate's position, including master on vessels 1,600 GT or below. This gets confusing because limited tonnage vessels still have the appointed positions like first or chief mate and second mate onboard, depending on the manning requirements of the vessel. It is only vessels more than 1,600 GT that have the specific ranks of third, second, and chief mates.

The last category is scope. This regulates the bodies of water in which the mariner can operate and where STCW applies. The recognized area of scope starts with the water closest to U.S. shores, labeled Inland Waters, Great Lakes, or Rivers, which is any water inside the Collision Regulations Line of Demarcation, outlining all U.S. inland waters. Each of these categories has a license scheme outlined in this book. The scope one step further would be Near Coastal, which signifies waters up to two hundred NM from U.S. shores, including inland waters. These licenses are used for coastal transport vessels, like a tug that moves barges from Long Beach, California, to San Francisco, California. The tug is transiting Inland and Near Coastal waters.

The last scope covers all bodies of water and is labeled Oceans. This scope includes the rest of the world's oceans, coasts, harbors, and waterways.

The rank, tonnage, and scope matrix can be in almost any combination, and the mariner's sea time dictates which license or document they receive. MMDs work the same way for ABs, which have tonnage and water restrictions based on the types of sea time.

One of the issues in the licensing scheme from the Coast Guard is the equivalencies of licenses. For example, a second mate unlimited oceans also is qualified as a 1,600 GT master oceans. Based on sea time requirements, a 1,600 GT master also can qualify for a master of fishing vessels. These equivalencies are good to know because you want to attach everything you can to your license for marketability. You do not want to be the 1,600 ton master who could not take a second or third mate unlimited job because you did not know you qualified or test for it.

The sea service requirements are listed from Unlimited Master Oceans to Ordinary Seaman. All equivalencies are detailed for each license, so mariners know what they qualified for based on their sea time, and what type of sea time to obtain for each license they want. The license structure is detailed by tonnage of license, then scope of water, then rank of license. This section has been referenced from 46CFR part 10, *The Licensing of Maritime Personnel.* The CFR can be found onboard ship in paperback, CD ROM, or on the CFR Web site at: www.access.gpo.gov/nara/cfr/index. html. Each license and document has a specific requirement, but the licensing scheme has both equivalencies and restrictions. For the Coast Guard's purpose, one year of sea time equals 360 days.

Vessels of Any Gross Tons/Unlimited (All Vessels More Than 1,600 GT)

Sea time for unlimited (more than 1,600 GT) ocean and near coastal, inland, and Great Lakes licenses must adhere to the 46CFR 10.402 and 10.430 requirements, which state that: *All* the required experience (sea time) *must* be on steam or motor vessels of over 200 GT, and that *at least half* of the required experience (sea time) *must* be on steam or motor vessels over 1600 GT.

The italicized words emphasize the scheme. If the scheme is not followed, the Coast Guard could refuse the sea time as credible or place tonnage restrictions on the license, meaning you could not serve in the capacity of your license on unlimited ships until the restrictions are lifted by fulfilling the sea time requirements sailing as a lower rank on the appropriate tonnage vessel. Again, this format must be followed for *all unlimited tonnage licenses.*

This outline is intended to help mariners understand what kind of sea time is needed, so that no time is wasted on vessels that do not help advancement. It is important to ask what the vessel's registered tonnage and routes are and make sure those are valid before signing on for an extended period of time. Here is a tip to make sure the vessel qualifies. Go to the USCG Web site, http://cgmix.uscg.mil/PSIX/VesselSearch.aspx, and enter the vessel's information. If the vessel is registered in the United States, this site will give the gross tonnage and other information on the vessel. Be specific. Enter as much information as possible: IMO number, hull number, call sign, etc., to make sure you are searching for the right vessel.

The unlimited tonnage licenses are listed by scope or bodies of water, then rank, starting at the highest ranking license. Scope increases by: "U.S. Rivers," "Inland Waters," "Great Lakes and Inland Waters," "Near Coastal Waters," and "Oceans or Near Coastal Waters combined." Each scope or body of water requires the mariner to sail it to be qualified. Each raise in scope includes all the previous U.S. bodies of water.

Oceans or Near Coastal Waters (Any Gross Tons) 46CFR 10.402

The important thing to remember with the oceans and near coastal licenses is sea time requirements have the words "ocean or near coastal" in them. This means that the proof of sea time, along with the tonnage requirements, better have those words or something similar, like "Coastwise" or "Foreign" routes, so the Coast Guard does not question if the sea time was acquired on the appropriate waters. Remember the sea time scheme for unlimited tonnage requires only half of the sea time to be more than 1,600 GT, and all sea time to be more than 200 GT.

Master, Any Gross Tons 46CFR 10.404

"a. A minimum of one year as chief mate on ocean or near coastal steam or motor vessels; or,

b. One year of service on ocean steam or motor vessels while holding a license as chief mate of ocean steam or motor vessels as follows:

1. (A minimum of six months of service as a chief mate; and

2. Service as an officer in charge of a navigational watch [OIC-NW] accepted on a two-for-one basis (12 months as second or third mate equals six months of credible service)."

Ranking is self explanatory. A candidate must have at least six months' service as a chief mate, coupled with an additional year as a second or third mate serving as OICNW while holding a chief mate license on the appropriate tonnage vessel, or serve as a chief mate for one year total. Remember the tonnage scheme.

Chief Mate, Any Gross Tons 46CFR 10.405

"The minimum service required to qualify an applicant for license as chief mate of ocean or near coastal steam or motor vessels of any gross tons is one year of service as officer in charge of a navigational watch on ocean steam or motor vessels while holding a license as second mate."

This means you can serve as mate on any vessel under 1,600 GT as long as you have the second mate's license while doing so. Just like the example above for master, a second mate unlimited can serve as master, chief mate, or second mate on vessels more than 200 GT, assuming the equivalency master's tests have been passed, *or* the mariner has served as a third or second mate on vessels more than 1,600 GT. I know it is confusing, but it will become clearer the more sea experience you obtain.

Second Mate, Any Gross Tons 46CFR 10.406

"One year of service as officer in charge of a navigational watch on ocean steam or motor vessels while holding a license as a third mate of ocean or near coastal; *or,* While holding a license as third mate; or (B) A minimum of six months' service as officer in charge of a navigational watch on ocean steam or motor vessels in combination with service on ocean or motor vessels as boatswain, able seaman, or quartermaster (helmsman) while holding a certificate as able seaman, which may be accepted on a two-for-one basis to a maximum allowable substitution of six months (12 months of experience (sea time) equals six months of credible service)."

This means that following the tonnage scheme for unlimited licenses, a third mate unlimited can serve up to twelve months as an AB and six months as a third mate and qualify for a second mate license.

Equivalencies: A licensed master of Great Lakes and inland steam or motor vessels of unlimited tonnage may obtain an unlimited second mate's license of Ocean or Near Coastal waters by completing the prescribed examination.

An unlimited second mate of Ocean or Near Coastal waters is eligible for a master's license of vessels not more than 1,600 GT upon Ocean or Near Coastal waters upon completion of the prescribed examination.

Third Mate, Any Gross Tons 46CFR 10.407

"Three years' (1080 days) service in the deck department on ocean steam or motor vessels, *six months* of which will have been as able seaman, boatswain, or quartermaster (helmsman), while holding a certificate as able seaman. Experience (sea time) gained in the engine department on vessels *of appropriate tonnage* may be credible for up to three months of the service requirements for this license. Or graduation from a maritime or military academy with appropriate qualifications from that academy."

Equivalencies: 1,600 ton ocean and near coastal master license serving twelve *months* as a *master* on an ocean or near coastal vessel more than 200 GT will qualify for a third mate unlimited oceans license. A third mate unlimited oceans qualifies for 100 ton inland master, no exam required.

Great Lakes and Inland Waters (Any Gross Tons)

The unlimited tonnage format does not change, only the bodies of water (scope). The important thing in this category is the difference between the Great Lakes and Inland Waters. 46CFR 10.430 states, "Any license issued for service on Great Lakes *and* inland waters is valid on all of the inland waters of the United States. Any license issued for service on *inland waters only* is valid for the inland waters of the United States, *excluding the Great Lakes.*

"Licenses with either Great Lakes and Inland Waters or Inland Waters only are valid for service on the sheltered waters in the Inside Passage between Puget Sound and Cape Spencer, Alaska. These licenses authorize service on waters seaward (outside) the (COLREGS) demarcation line as defined in 33CFR80, the applicant *must* complete an examination on the COLREGS, or the license must be endorsed with an exclusion from such waters."

This means you must pass an additional test from the USCG before you can transit outside COLREGS through the inside passage. COLREGS is a line of demarcation drawn by the USCG to signify the separation of international waters and the respective navigational rules, and U.S. inland waters and the respective rules. Mariners transiting both waters must be proficient in both sets of navigational rules. COLREGS stands for the Convention on the International Regulations for Preventing Collisions at Sea, 1972.

Master, Any Gross Tons and Inland 46CFR 10.433

"One year of service as mate or first class pilot while acting in the capacity of first mate of Great Lakes steam or motor vessels of more than 1600 GT, or at least six months of service as mate or first class pilot while acting in the capacity of first mate (over 1600 GT), including 12 additional months serving in the capacity of second mate on a two-for-one basis (12 months service = 6 months credible service)."

Equivalencies: Two years of service as master of Inland Waters, excluding Great Lakes, of steam or motor vessels more than 1,600 GT. A first class pilot is a designated person hired for their local knowledge of a specific area. They usually are confined to that area—a harbor, lake, or river—and help ships transit those areas. Almost every major harbor in the world has pilots that control shipping. The qualifications to become a pilot are extensive and I do not cover them in this book. If you plan on becoming a pilot, talk to your USCG REC about what you need to do.

Master, Any Gross Tons (Inland Only) 46CFR 10.435

"One year of service as first class pilot (other than canal and small lakes routes) or mate of Great Lakes or inland steam or motor vessels of more than 1600 GT.

Or two years of service as wheelsman (helmsman) or quartermaster while holding a mate/first class pilot license."

Note that the year of service as a mate or first class pilot must be on vessels more than 1,600 GT. For the two years as a wheelsman (helmsman) or quartermaster while holding a mate/pilot license, I would keep consistent with tonnage requirements and make sure that all of it is on vessels more than 1,600 GT.

Mate, Any Gross Tons (Great Lakes and Inland) 46CFR 10.437

"Three years' service (sea time) in the deck department of steam or motor vessels, at three months of which *must* have been on vessels upon inland waters (including Great Lakes) and at least six months *must* have been as an able seaman, inland mate, boatswain, wheelsman, quartermaster (helmsman), or equivalent position. Or, graduation from the Great Lakes Maritime Academy with appropriate qualifications."

Equivalencies: One year of service as a master of vessels over 200 GT while holding a license as master of Great Lakes and inland waters of not more than 1,600 GT

Rivers
Master or Mate of Rivers, Any Gross Tons
46CFR 10.459

"An applicant for license as master of river steam or motor vessels of any gross tons (unlimited) *must* meet the same service requirements as master of inland waters only steam or motor vessels of any gross tons. Service on the Great Lakes is not, however, required."

An applicant for mate, any gross tons, upon rivers must follow the guidelines set forth in CFR 10.437, which is mate, any gross tons (inland and Great Lakes).

Vessels of Not More Than 1,600 Gross Tons
Oceans or Near Coastal Waters
46CFR 10.412

The checklists for Master 500 ton Ocean/Near Coastal and Master 1,600 ton ocean/near coastal *do not* match the CFR sea time requirements. The USCG and NMC are aware of the problems and are working to fix them. Make sure you are aware of these discrepancies, and any that you see on the USCG Web site can be posted on the *New Hawsepipe* Web site (www.thenewhawsepipe. com). That way, mariners can benefit from the information.

Master, Not More Than 1600 GT 46CFR 10.412
Oceans or Near Coastal Waters

This license has a lot of stipulations, which means you can qualify many different ways. Be mindful of the tonnage requirements and sea service time matrix.

"Four years of total service (sea time) is required on ocean or near coastal waters (although service on Great Lakes and inland waters can be credible for up to two years of the total four required).

Two years of service *must* have been on vessels more than 100 GT.

Two years of service *must* be as a master, mate, master, or mate of towing vessels, or equivalent supervisory position. Within this service, one year *must* be on vessels more than 100 GT."

Equivalencies: Chief mate unlimited oceans and second mate unlimited oceans are eligible for this license upon completion of a limited exam.

Mate, Not More Than 1600 GT 46CFR 10.414
Oceans or Near Coastal Waters

"Three years' total service (sea time) in the deck department of ocean or near coastal steam, motor, sail or auxiliary sail vessels. Service (sea time) on the Great Lakes and inland waters may be substituted for up to 18 *months.*

One year of service *must* have been on vessels over 100 GT.

One year of service *must* have been as a master, mate, master or mate of towing vessels, or equivalent supervisory position *while holding a license* as master, mate, master or mate of towing vessels or equivalent supervisory position. Six months of this service *must* have been on vessels over 100 GT. *Or,* three years' total service (sea time) in the deck department on ocean or near coastal steam or motor, sail or auxiliary sail vessels of over 200 GT. Six months of this service *must* have been as an able seaman."

Near Coastal Waters *Only*

This is a special category, limiting the mariner to inland waters, including Great Lakes and within two hundred NM miles of U.S. coastline. A mariner's sea time does not have to be just on near coastal waters. This license merely requires a shorter amount of sea time from oceans to inland.

Mate, Not More Than 1,600 GT 46CFR 10.416
(Near Coastal *Only*)

"Two years total service in the deck dept. of ocean or near coastal steam, motor, sail or auxiliary sail vessels. Service on the Great Lakes and inland waters may be substituted for up to *one year* of the required service (sea time). One year of the required service (sea time) *must* have been on vessels over 100 GT and six months of the required service (sea time) *must* have been as able seaman, boatswain, quartermaster, or equivalent supervisory position on vessels over 100 GT while *holding a certificate as able seaman."*

Great Lakes and Inland Waters

The important thing in this category is the difference between the Great Lakes *and* Inland waters. 46CFR 10.430 states, "Any license issued for service on Great Lakes and inland waters is valid on all of the inland waters of the United States. Any license issued for service on *inland waters only* is valid for the inland waters of the United States, *excluding the Great Lakes."*

Master, Not More Than 1,600 GT 46CFR 10.442 (Great Lakes and Inland Waters)

"Three years' total service on vessels. 18 *months* of the required service (sea time) *must* have been on vessels of over 100 GT. One year of the required service (sea time) *must* have been as a master, mate or equivalent supervisory position on vessels over 100 GT *while holding a license* as master, mate, or as master of towing vessels. Or, six months of service as operator on vessels over 100 GT *while holding a license as master of towing vessels."*

Mate, Not More Than 1,600 GT 46CFR 10.444 (Great Lakes and Inland Waters)

"Two years' total service (sea time) in the deck department of steam or motor, sail or auxiliary sail vessels. One year of the required service (sea time) *must* have been on vessels over 100 GT and *six months* of the required service (sea time) *must* have been as able seaman, boatswain, quartermaster, or equivalent position on vessels over 100 GT *while holding a certificate as able seaman.* Or, one year total service (sea time) as master of steam or motor, sail or auxiliary sail vessels, or operator of uninspected passenger vessels, of over 50 GT *while holding a license* as master of steam or motor, sail or auxiliary sail vessels of not more than 200 GT or operator of uninspected passenger vessels. Or, six months' total service (sea time) as mate of towing vessels over 100 GT."

Rivers 46CFR 10.459

"An applicant for a license as master or mate of river steam or motor vessels with a limitation of 25-1600 GT *must* meet the *same service requirements* as those required for the corresponding tonnage Great Lakes and inland steam or motor license. Service on the Great Lakes is not, however, required."

In this case, the corresponding tonnage would be master or mate of vessels not over 1600 GT, Great Lakes and inland waters.

Vessels of Not More Than 500 Gross Tons
Oceans or Near Coastal Waters
Master, Not More Than 500 GT 46CFR 10.418
(Oceans or Near Coastal Waters)

"Three years' total service (sea time) on ocean or near coastal waters. Service (sea time) on Great Lakes and inland waters can be substituted for up to 18 months of the required service. *Two years must* have been as a master, mate or equivalent supervisory position *while holding a license* as master, mate, or operator of uninspected passenger vessels. One year of this required service *must* have been on vessels over 50 GT."

Equivalencies: A master or mate of towing vessels authorizing service on oceans or near coastal routes is eligible for a license as master of ocean or near coastal routes of not more than five hundred GT after serving one year as a master or mate of towing vessels on oceans or near coastal routes *and* completion of a limited exam.

Mate, Not More Than 500 Gross Tons 46CFR 10.420
(Oceans and Near Coastal Waters)

"Two years' total service in the deck department on ocean or near coastal steam or motor, sail or auxiliary sail vessels. Service on the Great Lakes and inland waters may be substituted for up to one year of the required service. One year of the required service (sea time) *must* have been as a master, mate, or equivalent supervisory position while holding a license as a master, mate, or operator of uninspected passenger vessels. *Six months* of that licensed service *must* be on vessels of over 50 GT."

Mate, Not More Than 500 Gross Tons 46CFR 10.421

"Two years total service in the deck department of ocean or near coastal steam or motor, sail or auxiliary sail vessels. Service on Great Lakes and inland waters can be substituted for up to one year of service. *One year* of service *must* have been on vessels of over 50 GT. *Three months* of service *must* have been as able seaman, boatswain, quartermaster, or equivalent position on vessels of over 50 GT *while holding* a certificate as able seaman."

Great Lakes and Inland Waters

The important thing in this category is the difference between the Great Lakes *and* Inland waters. 46CFR 10.430 states, "Any license issued for service on Great Lakes and inland waters is valid on all of the inland waters of the United States. Any license issued for service on *inland waters only* is valid for the inland waters of the United States, *excluding the Great Lakes.*"

Master, Not More Than 500 Gross Tons 46CFR 10.446 (Great Lakes and Inland Waters)

"Three years total service on vessels. One year required service *must* have been as master, mate, or equivalent supervisory position on vessels over 50 GT *while holding* a license as master, mate, or operator of uninspected passenger vessels.

Equivalencies: A licensed master of ocean, near coastal, Great Lakes, or inland *towing vessels* is eligible for this license after *six months'* service as a *master of towing vessels* and completion of a limited exam. Two of the three years needed *must* have been while holding a license as master, mate of towing vessels, or mate.

Mate, Not More Than 500 Gross Tons 46CFR 10.448 (Great Lakes and Inland Waters)

"Two years' total service (sea time) in the deck department of steam or motor, sail or auxiliary sail vessels of over 50 GT. Three months of the required service *must* have been as able seaman, boatswain, quartermaster, or equivalent position on vessels over 50 GT *while holding* a certificate as able seaman."

Rivers 46CFR 10.459

"An applicant for a license as master or mate of river steam or motor vessels with a limitation of 25-1600 GT *must* meet the *same service requirements* as those required for the corresponding tonnage Great Lakes and inland steam or motor license."

In this case, master and mates of not more than 500 GT.

Vessels of Not More Than 200 Gross Tons
Oceans and Near Coastal Waters
Master, Not More Than 200 Gross Tons 46CFR 10.424

"Three years total service on ocean or near coastal waters. Service on Great Lakes and inland waters may substitute for up to 18 months of the required service. *Two years* of the required service *must* have been as master, mate, or equivalent supervisory position *while holding* a license as master, mate or operator of un-inspected passenger vessels. *Or, two years'* total service as licensed master or mate of ocean or near coastal *towing vessels,* including completion of a *limited exam."*

Addition: If the mariner wishes to obtain an endorsement of sail or auxiliary sail on this license, evidence of 12 *months'* service on sail or auxiliary sail vessels *must* be submitted.

Near Coastal Waters *Only*
Master, Not More Than 200 Gross Tons 46CFR 10.426

"Two years' service (sea time) on ocean or near coastal waters. Service on Great Lakes and inland waters *may* substitute for up to *one year* of the required service. *One year* of the required service *must* have been as master, mate or equivalent supervisory position *while holding* a license as master, mate or operator of unin-spected passenger vessels. *Or, one year* of total service as licensed master or mate of *towing vessels* on oceans or near coastal routes, *including completion of a limited exam."*

Addition: To obtain an additional endorsement for sail of aux-iliary sail on this license, evidence of 12 *months'* service on sail or auxiliary sail vessels *must* be submitted.

Mate, Not More Than 200 Gross Tons 46CFR 10.427
(Near Coastal Waters Only)

"One year total service on deck of ocean or near coastal steam or motor, sail or auxiliary sail vessels. Service on Great Lakes and inland waters *may* be substituted for up to *six months* of the re-quired service. Or, *three months* of service operating on any waters *while holding* a license as master of inland steam or motor, sail or auxiliary sail vessels of not more than 200 GT."

Additions: Sail or auxiliary sail endorsements can be obtained by submitting evidence of *six months'* service on sail or auxiliary sail vessels.

Equivalencies: Operator of uninspected passenger vessels with a near coastal route endorsement may obtain this license by completing the required limited examination on rules and regulations of small passenger vessels.

Great Lakes and Inland Waters
Master, Not More Than 200 Gross Tons 46CFR 10.452

"One year of service (sea time) on vessels. *Six months* of the required service *must* have been as master, mate, master or mate of towing vessels, or equivalent supervisory position *while holding* a license as master, mate, master or mate of towing vessels, or operator of uninspected passenger vessels. To obtain authority to serve on the Great Lakes, *three months* of the required service *must* have been on the Great Lakes. Otherwise, the license will be limited to inland waters of the U.S. *only* (excluding Great Lakes)."

Addition: To obtain an endorsement for sail or auxiliary sail for this license, an applicant *must* have *six months* of service on sail or auxiliary sail vessels.

Mate, Not More Than 200 Gross Tons 46CFR 10.454
(Great Lakes and Inland Waters)

"Six months of service (sea time) in the deck department of steam or motor, sail or auxiliary sail vessels. To obtain authority to serve on the Great Lakes, *three months* of the required service *must* have been on Great Lakes waters. Otherwise, the license will be limited to inland waters of the U.S. *only* (excluding the Great Lakes)."

Addition: To obtain the sail or auxiliary sail endorsement, *three months* of service *must* have been on sail or auxiliary sail vessels.

Equivalencies: An operator of uninspected passenger vessels may obtain this license by successfully completing an examination on rules and regs for small passenger vessels. The Great Lakes requirements still stand *(three months).*

Rivers 46CFR 10.459

"An applicant for a license as master or mate of river steam or motor vessels with a limitation of 25-1600 GT *must* meet the *same service requirements* as those required for the corresponding tonnage Great Lakes and inland steam or motor license."

In this case, master and mates of not more than 200 GT.

Vessels Not More Than 100 Gross Tons
Near Coastal Waters Only
Master, Not More Than 100 Gross Tons 46CFR 10.428

"Two years working in the deck department total on steam or motor, sail or auxiliary sail vessels on *ocean or near coastal waters.* Service on Great Lakes and inland water may be substituted for up to one year of the required service."

Additional: To obtain a sail or auxiliary sail endorsement on this license, the applicant must submit evidence of 12 *months'* service on sail or auxiliary sail vessels.

Limited Master, Not More Than 100 Gross Tons
46CFR 10.429 (Near Coastal Waters Only)

"Four months of service on any waters on vessels for which the license is requested. This license is usually issued to mariners employed by yacht clubs, marinas, formal camps and educational institutions. A license issued under this section is *limited to the specific activity and locality* of the above employers."

Additional: The applicant must complete an USCG-approved Safe Boating Course and a limited examination including First Aid and CPR. To obtain a sail or auxiliary sail endorsement, four months' service on sail or auxiliary sail vessels *must* be submitted.

Great Lakes and Inland Waters
Master, Not More Than 100 Gross Tons 46CFR 10.455

"One Year of total service (sea time) in the deck department of steam or motor, sail or auxiliary sail vessels. To obtain authority to serve on the Great Lakes, *three months* of the total service *must* be obtained on Great Lakes waters. Otherwise, the license will be restricted to inland waters of the U.S. only (excluding the Great Lakes)."

Additional: To obtain a sail or auxiliary sail endorsement, *six months* of the total service *must* be on sail or auxiliary sail vessels.

Limited Master, Not More Than 100 Gross Tons 46CFR 10.456 (Great Lakes and Inland Waters)

"Four months of service on any waters on vessels for which the license is requested. This license is usually issued to mariners employed by yacht clubs, marinas, formal camps and educational institutions. A license issued under this section is *limited to the specific activity and locality* of the above employers."

Additional: The applicant must complete a USCG-approved Safe Boating Course and a limited examination including First Aid and CPR. To obtain a sail or auxiliary sail endorsement, four months' service on sail or auxiliary sail vessels *must* be submitted.

Inland Waters Only
Master, Not More Than 100 Gross Tons 46CFR 10.457

"One Year of service on *any waters.*"

Additional: To obtain a sail or auxiliary sail endorsement, six months of the required service must be on sail or auxiliary vessels.

Rivers 46CFR 10.459

"An applicant for a license as master or mate of river steam or motor vessels with a limitation of 25-1600 GT *must* meet the *same service requirements* as those required for the corresponding tonnage Great Lakes and inland steam or motor license."

In this case, master and mates of not more than 100 GT.

Licenses for Certain Industries

Fishing
Master, Uninspected Fishing Vessels Over 1,600 Gross Tons, But Not More Than 5000 Gross Tons 46CFR 10.462

"Four years' total service on ocean or near coastal routes. Service on Great Lakes or inland waters *may* substitute for up to *two years* of the required service. *Two years* of service *must* have been on vessels over 100 gross tons, and *one year must* have been as a licensed master, mate or equivalent on vessels over 100 gross tons *while holding* a license as master, mate, master or mate of towing vessels OR operator of uninspected passenger vessels."

The tonnage of the license depends on the size of the vessels the *four years* of qualifying sea time was acquired. The license will be limited to the maximum tonnage on which 25% (one year) of the required service was obtained. The tonnage limitations are in 1000 gross ton increments, starting at 1600 and going up to, but not exceeding 5000 gross tons. Depending, again, on the maximum tonnage that was sailed on for at least *one year.*

Master, Uninspected Fishing Vessels Not More Than 1,600 Gross Tons 46CFR 10.462

"Four years total service on ocean or near coastal routes. Service on Great Lakes or inland waters *may* substitute for up to *two years* of the required service. Two years of service *must* have been on vessels over 100 gross tons, and *one year must* have been as a licensed master, mate or equivalent on vessels over 100 gross tons *while holding* a license as master, mate, master or mate of towing vessels *or* operator of uninspected passenger vessels."

Master, Uninspected Fishing Vessels Not More Than 500 Gross Tons 46CFR 10.462

"Four years total service on ocean or near coastal routes. Service on Great Lakes or inland waters *may* substitute for up to *two years* of the required service. *Two years* of service *must* have been on vessels over 50 gross tons, and *one year must* have been as a licensed master, mate or equivalent on vessels over 50 gross tons *while holding* a license as master, mate, master or mate of towing vessels *or* operator of uninspected passenger vessels."

Mate, Uninspected Fishing Vessels Over 1,600 Gross Tons, But Not More Than 5000 Gross Tons 46CFR 10.462

"*Three years'* total service on ocean or near coastal routes. Service (sea time) on Great Lakes or inland waters may substitute for up to 18 *months* of the required service. The license will be limited to the maximum tonnage on which at least 25 % of the required service was obtained.

To qualify for a license of not more than 1,600 gross tons, at least *one year* of the required service *must* have been on vessels over 100 gross tons.

To qualify for a license of not more than 500 gross tons, at least *one year* of the required service *must* have been on vessels over 50 gross tons."

Towing Vessels 46CFR 10.463
"A license issued to an officer of towing vessels does not authorize service aboard such vessels on a foreign voyage nor aboard vessels greater than 200 gross tons on ocean or near coastal waters. The Coast Guard issues the following licenses:
- Master of towing vessels
- Master of towing vessels, harbor assist
- Master of towing vessels, limited (less than 200 gross tons and restricted to a local inland area)
- Mate (Pilot) of towing vessels
- Mate (Pilot) of towing vessels, limited (less than 200 gross tons and restricted to a local inland area)
- Apprentice mate
- Apprentice mate, harbor assist
- Apprentice mate, limited (less than 200 gross tons and restricted to a local inland area)"

On the following pages are the tables from 46CFR Part 10 detailing the requirements for towing licenses. Be careful to look at the right table: master, mate, or apprentice. Look also at the Towing Officer's Assessment Record (TOAR) and assessment requirements following these tables.

The TOAR is a list of practical tasks the hawsepiper must perform to obtain a towing officer's license. The detail of the record also is in chapter six, under practical assessments.

Uninspected Passenger Vessels (Six Pack) 46CFR 10.467
"a. This section applies to all applicants for the license to operate an uninspected vessel of less than 100 gross tons, equipped with propulsion machinery of any type, carrying six or less passengers.

b. Operator of uninspected passenger vessels licenses issued for ocean waters will be limited to near coastal waters not more than 100 miles offshore. Licenses issued for inland waters will include all inland waters, except Great Lakes. Licenses may be issued for a particular local area under paragraph (g) of this section.

Table 3.1. Requirements for license as master of towing vessels[3]

1. Route Endorsed	2. Total Service[2]	3. TOS[3] on T/V as Mate (Pilot)	4. TOS[3] on T/V as Mate (Pilot) Not as Harbor Assist	5. TOS[3] on Particular Route	6. Subordinate Route Authorized
(1) Ocean	48	18 of 48	12 of 18	3 of 18	NC, GL - 1
(2) Near-Coastal (NC)	48	18 of 48	12 of 18	3 of 18	GL - 1
(3) Great Lakes-Inland (GL-1)	48	18 of 48	12 of 18	3 of 18	
(4) Western Rivers (WR)	48	18 of 48	12 of 18	3 of 18	

1. If you hold a licenseas master of towing vessels you may have an endorsement -- as mate [pilot] of towing vessels for a route superior to your current route on which you have no operating experience -- placed on your license after passing an examination for that additional route. After you complete 90 days of experience and complete a TOAR on that route, we will add it to your license as master of towing vessels and remove the one for mate (pilot) of towing vessels.
2. Service is in months.
3. TOS is time of service.

Table 3.2. Requirements for license as mate (pilot[1]) of towing vessesls

	1. Route Endorsed	2. Total Service[2]	3. TOS[3] on T/V as Appretice Mate (Steersman)	4. TOS[3] on Particular Route	5. TOAR[4] or an Approved Course	6. 30 Day of Observation and Training while Holding Master (Limited) and Pass a Limited Examination	7. Subordiante Route Authorized
(1) Ocean		30	12 of 30	3 of 12	Yes	Yes	NC, GL - 1
(2) Near-Coastal (NC)		30	12 of 30	3 of 12	Yes	Yes	GL - 1
(3) Great Lakes-Inland (GL-1)		30	12 of 48	3 of 12	Yes	Yes	
(4) Western Rivers (WR)		30	12 of 48	3 of 12	Yes	No (90 days service required)	

1. For all inland routes, as well as Western Rivers, the license as pilot of towing vessels is equivalent to that as mate of towing vessels. All qualifications and qquivalencies are the same.
2. Service is in months unless otherwise indicated.
3. TOS is time of service.
4. TOAR is Towing Officers' Assessment Record.

Table 3.3. Requirements for license as apprentice mate (steersman) of towing vessels

1. Licence Type	2. Route Endorsed	3. Total Service[1]	4. TOS[2] on T/V	5. TOS[2] on Particular Route	6. Pass Examination[3]
(1) Apprentice Mate (Steersman)	Ocean (O)	18	12 of 18	3 of 18	Yes
	Near-Coast (NC)	18	12 of 18	3 of 18	Yes
	Great-Lakes Inland (GL-1)	18	12 of 18	3 of 18	Yes
	Western Rivers (WR)	18	12 of 18	3 of 18	Yes
(4) Western Rivers (WR)	Not Applicable	18	12 of 18	3 of 18	Yes

1. Service in months.
2. TOS is time of service.
3. The examination for apprentice mate is specified in subpart I of this part. The examination for apprentice mate (limited) is a limited examination.
4. For all inland routes, as well Western Rivers, teh license as steersman is equivalent to that as apprentice mate. All qualifications and equivalencies are the same.

c. For a license as operator of an uninspected passenger vessel with a near coastal endorsement, an applicant must have a minimum of 12 months experience in the operation of vessels, including at least three months service on vessels operating on ocean or near coastal waters.

d. For a license as operator of an uninspected passenger vessel with a Great Lakes and inland waters endorsement, an applicant must have 12 months service on Great Lakes or inland waters, including at least three months service operating vessels on Great Lakes waters.

e. For a license as operator of an uninspected passenger vessel with an inland endorsement, an applicant must have a minimum of 12 months experience in the operation of vessels.

f. An operator of uninspected passenger vessels license, limited on its face to undocumented vessels, may be issued to a person who is not a citizen of the United States.

g. Limited operator of uninspected passenger vessel licenses may be issued to applicants to be employed by organizations such as formal camps, yacht clubs, educational institutions, and marinas. A license issued under this paragraph will be limited to the specific activity and the locality of the camp, yacht club, or marina. In order to obtain this restricted license, an applicant must:

　1. Have three months service in the operation of the type of vessel for which the license is requested; and,

　2. Satisfactorily complete a safe boating course approved by the National Association of State Boating Law Administrators, or those public education courses conducted by the U.S. Power Squadron or the American National Red Cross or a Coast Guard approved course; and,

　3. Pass a limited examination appropriate for the activity to be conducted and the route authorized.

　4. The first aid and cardiopulmonary resuscitation (CPR) course certificates required by Sec. 10.205(h) of this part will only be required when, in the opinion of the OCMI, the geographic area over which service is authorized precludes obtaining medical services within a reasonable time.

h. An applicant for a license as operator of uninspected passenger vessels who intends to serve only in the vicinity of Puerto Rico, and who speaks Spanish only, may be issued a license restricted to the navigable waters of the United States in the vicinity of Puerto Rico."

Merchant Mariner Documents (Unlicensed)

Able-Bodied Seaman (AB)

ABs make up most of the deck gang onboard ships. They are the go-everywhere, do-everything kind of person onboard.

There are several types of ABs. The sea time and restrictions differ for each one. The term "deck service" in each of the sea time requirements for AB is defined as, "Service in the deck department in work related to the work usually performed onboard vessels by Able Seaman." (46 United States Code [USC] 7301).

All the sea service requirements for ABs and OSs are taken from the 46CFR Part 12, Certification of Seaman. The progression to AB is time gained while serving as an OS or deckhand onboard. Some ships rotate new comers through all the departments: deck, engine and stewarding, to find out what job fits the mariner best. Sea service for AB can come from different departments, as this is the first step in the hawsepipe: OS to AB.

AB has tonnage requirements and scope, like officer licenses. They are: Unlimited, Limited, Special, Sail, and Offshore Supply Vessel.

AB (Unlimited)

"1080 days (3 years) deck service on oceans or Great Lakes."

Sounds simple enough, but it does take a while. If you are going for an unlimited AB it is a good career, but it could be only the beginning. Unlimited ABs require the same amount of sea time as a third mate unlimited. Think about that. You can be taking the classes required for third mate during your breaks as an AB while acquiring the sea time toward it. This is the preferred method. Make the decision to advance and then work toward it by gaining the sea time and certificates as you go.

Also, if you are upgrading from limited to unlimited, the 540 days you already have will count, but at least 18 months must be on vessels of 1,600 GT or more (if you do not have it already), so keep that in mind. Mainers also need BST, Life Boatman, and Ratings Forming Part of a Navigational Watch (RFPNW) to qualify for AB unlimited

AB (Limited)

"540 days (18 months) deck service on vessels of 100 GT or more, not exclusively confined to the rivers and smaller inland lakes of the U.S. (CFR)."

This means you can get your sea time anywhere, but it has to be on vessels greater than 100 GT. It is work you can do on any waters, domestic or international. Again, international waters require BST, Life Boatman, and RFPNW for both domestic and international. If you are on an oceangoing and unlimited vessel as a limited AB, some masters will not permit any limited ABs to work as helmsmen or lookout while in pilotage waters. I have worked on vessels as an AB and a mate where this policy was in effect by the master. Hopefully it will not happen to you, but do not get discouraged if it does. I saw the eighty-three-year-old AB unlimited who did get to work as a helmsman, but could not hear one rudder command. He was always shouting, "What?" and I thought to myself, "Yeah, this is much safer than a limited or special AB who can hear."

No matter what opinion you or I have, it is up to the master of the vessel, and there are no arguments about it. Do not let this small stuff bother you. If you are a good helmsman you can always approach the master (using chain of command) with the request to steer in pilotage waters. I have said this before, the eagerness to learn should be rewarded; otherwise how else are you going to be a good helmsman? I have seen it happen. Masters have let OSs steer in pilotage waters shadowed by qualified ABs to get their RFPNW assessments signed off (chapter six). But it was not without a request to do so and proper training beforehand from the ABs and the mate on watch. Keep that in mind.

AB (Special)

"360 day (12 months) of deck service on oceans or navigable waters of the U.S, including the Great Lakes."

It is the first step of an OS to an AB. The manning requirements of vessels state that the deck crew can be made up of a mix of ABs. As long as a certain percentage of qualified ABs (limited or unlimited as the case may be) is among the deck crew, the rest can be made up of Specials. For most OSs, this is the quickest way to being an AB, which means more money, which is the name of the game. Some companies and maritime unions pay their ABs differently based on their endorsements. For example, an AB that has an unlimited endorsement gets paid the highest AB salary. AB limited gets paid a bit less, and an AB special even less. It is a mini-tier among the AB endorsements. I said some companies and unions, not all. Make sure you know the pay scale of the company or union regarding ABs' pay. Either way, it is better than OS pay, but you still do not want to be surprised.

For work as an AB special on international waters, STCW 95 Basic Safety Training, Life Boatman, and RFPNW assessments are required. In domestic inland waters, STCW does not apply, but you will still need RFPNW and lifeboat.

AB (Sail)

"180 days (6 months) 'deck service' on sailing school or equivalent sailing vessels on oceans or navigable waters of the U.S."

Make sure that you want to stay on sail vessels, as this MMD endorsement is limited to sailing vessels only. Also, for proof of sea service, make sure all the important information is on the letter or discharge, especially the fact that it is a sailing vessel. Like I said before, if the sailing vessel you work on is inland or domestic, an STCW 95 certificate is not required. If it is international, STCW 95 Basic Safety Training and Life Boatman are required. Always check with your company to see what you will need with your new AB ticket.

AB (Fishing)

"180 days (6 months) deck service (including fishing, fish processing and fish tenders) aboard oceans or navigable waters of the U.S. including the Great Lakes."

This also is a very restricting MMD. Fishing is an entity of its own, and if you plan to stay in it, this is all you might need. A lot of folks who work on fishing boats in the Gulf of Mexico or Alaska don't carry any documentation at all, being domestic and uninspected (also 100 GT and below).

I have known folks with years of fishing sea time who try to get AB MMDs without the required documentation. This happens because the fishing industry is sort of under the radar when it comes to vessel documentation. The majority of the fishing industry is not inspected by the USCG. For example, your uncle could have a small seiner and write you a letter saying you did twelve-hour days to get your AB sea time. I am not saying that this is not valid experience, but looking at it from a government organization, you can see that the fisherman is not going to have the certification and documentation the USCG is looking for. The USCG may not accept your sea time due to the nature of the work or the inability to verify. If you have good letters of sea time, they should accept them. I will talk more about the different ways to get sea time later in this chapter. Usually fishing vessels are inland or domestic. If that is the case, STCW 95 Basic Safety Training usually is not required. Always check with your company as to what you will need with your new AB MMD.

AB (Offshore Supply Vessels)
"180 days (6 months) deck service aboard oceans or navigable waters of the U.S. including the Great Lakes."

Offshore supply vessels (OSVs), like fishing vessels, have a similar uniqueness. They cater to the mobile, or fixed, offshore drilling stations, moving personnel and cargo, usually found in the Gulf of Mexico and Southern California. The boats usually are small (under 100 GT) and can go at a pretty good clip. Time is money to those folks, so they are gunning pretty hard, and it can get busy around some of the rigs. Some people make a good living at it, others have done it and hated it. I have spent some time down in the Gulf of Mexico and I did not mind it. It is hard work and long hours, especially when the weather is bad. But it is very educational and good experience is gained on deck.

Everyone has to find what they like in the maritime industry. Some even find a home "on the beach" working in a maritime office job. We need good people in the front offices as well as on the ships. Each person has a job. If we all do them well, the maritime industry can be one of the most exciting careers out there.

Ordinary Seaman (OS)
No sea time is required for this MMD. If you wish to sail on any oceangoing vessel, realize that OS is required to have STCW 95 Basic Safety Training. Remember, without the STCW 95 certificate you will be restricted to work on domestic vessels only. You want to qualify for AB as quickly as possible and not limit yourself to just domestic and near-coastal vessels, so I recommend getting the STCW 95 Basic Safety Training.

To find the checklists and applications for a new mariner, go to the USCG Merchant Mariner home page (http://www.uscg.

mil/stcw) and click on the left-hand side where it says "New Mariner's." A new box will appear. Click on "Where to begin" and the site will take you through a series of questions on what it is you want to do. Keep scrolling down, because a ton of information actually is there, including all the unlicensed union's info, schooling, and pay scales.

Contact *all* of the unions and nonunion companies on the list to get a clear picture of the job market. Ask each of them what additional endorsements, certificates, or fees are required to work for that company or union. Ask how much it will cost to get started and where to obtain the appropriate schooling. Have a good idea of what is ahead before you start the paperwork.

After that, go back to the "New Mariner" box on the USCG site and click on "General Package." This will give you all the information you need in the form of checklists that the USCG will require from you. Go back to the home page, click on the left-hand side where it says "Application and Downloads." A list of downloadable forms will appear. Click on the "Application for License or Merchant Mariner Document," and the application will appear (make sure the computer has Adobe Reader). Print it, fill it out, and bring it to the REC.

As an OS, make sure to get your AB RFPNW assessments signed either in the RFPNW class or onboard a vessel by a second mate or higher. This will be detailed in chapter six. Make sure you also get a "letter of watchstanding" (explained later in this chapter), or fill out a sea watch log, to leave no doubt in the Coast Guard's mind that you completed the assessments while underway.

Reference for All MMDs

The MMD is a credit card-sized government document that has your qualifications on the back of it. Your STCW certificate is a full page with your endorsements on it and your picture on the bottom. These two pieces of paper are the most important to your career. Keep them with you at all times.

If any of the above AB endorsements are what you are looking for (OSV, sail, fishing, special, limited, and unlimited), go to the USCG Merchant Mariner homepage (http://www.uscg.mil/stcw/). Go to the left-hand side and click "Info Packages." Click on "MMD Original or Endorsement with Qualified Ratings."

Make sure the computer you are working on has Abobe Reader software because all the forms from the Web site are PFD files, which requires Adobe Reader to view.

The page will list everything you need to obtain your document. Cross reference it with the information in this book as well as the company, union, or vessel you will be working on. You can never have enough information. If you find yourself in the USCG Web site home page, click on the left-hand side marked "Info Packages" and scroll down to "MMD Original or Endorsement with Qualified Ratings," then cut across and click on "Available." That will bring up the same documents you need. Any info packages and checklists you need for licenses can be found on the left-hand side labeled "checklists."

Sea Time

Accumulating sea time and documenting it is a long process. You can document it many different ways to, but you should be familiar with some unique qualities about it. The USCG loves to help the folks that come into the REC with all their documentation in order: official letterhead, tonnage, dates, times, duties performed, etc. Have an idea regarding what type of sea time you need. I don't know how many times I have talked to hawsepipers who think they have more sea time than they really do and are very disappointed after I explain to them the sea time is the wrong tonnage or scope.

For example, I have a friend who is working to be a third mate unlimited. When he first started thinking about it, he counted all the time he spent fishing and crabbing in Alaska and found he was only ninety days short of the total 1,080 days needed. Not true. I informed him, much to his dismay, all the boats he was on were 100 tons or less, and it specifically says that out of the 1,080 days at least eighteen months (540 days) *must* be spent on vessels more than 1,600 gross tons, and the rest of the time could be spent on vessels of *at least* 200 gross tons. You do not want to walk into the REC to apply for a license without knowing what kind of sea time you need and what kind you have.

Another example, you can have more than eighteen months (540) on vessels more than 1,600 gross tons. In fact, all of it can be on vessels more than 1,600 gross tons. The USCG is giving you some leeway in terms of tonnage. If you worked on a 500 ton coastal freighter or oceangoing tug, up to 540 days sea time could count toward your unlimited license. So many different kinds of deck licenses are available you really need to know what the USCG wants from you regarding sea time for your specific license. Once you start upgrading, the rules and regulations should become easier to read. The best way to get answers is to read the application forms for the license you desire, look at the USCG and CFR Web sites. Lastly, call or visit your local REC and ask them about your sea time and any other hypothetical scenarios I have not detailed in this book. Remember to ask someone. For example, I worked on a cruise ship as a steward but did deck-related duties too. Does any of that time count toward my license? How do I document it?

To document your sea service, the USCG requires you to provide a detailed letter or USCG discharge. Military personnel should follow the procedures listed in chapter nine. For civilian sea service letters, the Coast Guard will want as much information as possible. Marine companies usually are familiar with these documents, but do not entrust your well being to the company. Make sure the letters have everything the USCG requires. You would hate to get everything in order and then have the REC refuse your sea service letter because it was missing information. If you are in doubt, write it yourself and have the appropriate person sign it.

The general USCG application states that acceptable forms of sea service are:

An official USCG Certificate of Discharge is a small green sheet of paper given to you by the master of the vessel after completing a voyage. It is issued in triplicate. One copy is sent to USCG headquarters in Washington DC, one copy is kept by the vessel or company, and the original is given to you as verification of sea service. It has everything you need and is an official USCG document (CG-718A), so make sure you retain it and keep it with all the other important stuff. You will start to accumulate many of these as you gain sea time. Some "old timers" probably could wallpaper their houses with them, they have so many. Keep them all. Discharges and sea service letters also are used by companies and employment unions to verify medical benefits, vacation pay, continuing education and pension eligibility, so please, hang on to them.

Other official documents of sea service from marine companies can be original company letterhead signed by appropriate officials; usually the personnel officer, head of human resources, vessel owner, or licensed master. At minimum, the contents of the letter *must* include:

- Name and official number of each vessel on which the service was obtained. (If it is a particular vessel, i.e., sailing, OSV, make sure it states that as well).
- Vessel's gross tonnage, which we know is needed for any license upgrading.
- Number of days on each vessel including the dates of service. Usually this will be the dates you signed on and off the vessel, or for the case of tugs, a whole number of days throughout a given period when you actually were underway while working for the company.
- Number of underway days spent on each route, i.e., Oceans, Near Coastal, Inland, Western Rivers, Great Lakes.
- Number of hours worked per day (see day-and-a-half sea time).
- A brief description of duties or worked performed (letter of watchstanding).

Letters of Watchstanding

Under Policy letter [01-02], section 5-SEA SERVICE, part (a) it states, "Applicants must present evidence of three years sea service which includes six months service performing bridge watchkeeping duties under the supervision of a qualified master or licensed officer."

This means you should prove that at least six months (you can have more) of your AB time was spent as a part of the navigational watchstanding bridge team. When you get your discharge or proof of sea service letter, get an additional letter stating the watchstanding time. Most officers are unfamiliar with this additional letter. For your sake, have the policy letter handy and point the requirement out. Then add that there are many different types of ABs: day workers, maintenance, shore side standby, boatswain, watchstander, and the sea service discharge or letter does not always reflect which AB duties you are doing. This additional letter does that for the Coast Guard. I would draft the letter myself onboard, or get a supervisor to do it, though they might not have the time to help. Use the dates of your discharge or sea service letter and write it verbatim from the policy letter. The final draft should be on ship's or company letterhead. Try to get the ship's stamp on it if it is available.

Here is a sample:

> To Whom It May Concern:
> This letter is to certify that AB (or OS) Leonard W. Lambert (social security number) performed watch-standing duties as part of the bridge team under the master or qualified officers from (dates to reflect discharge) while onboard the (ship's name).
>
> Regards,
> Captain or Chief Mate

Day-and-a-half Sea Time

Some facets of the industry work seasonally, such as fishing, tour, and charter. What mariners in these fields tried to do with the USCG was say in effect, "We work as much as we can in short periods of time. During this time, we have no set schedules and we work until the job is done. By definition, one 'sea day' is comprised of eight hours. We work twelve to sixteen hours a day, sometimes more, or we are on six-hour watch rotations. We would like to be compensated for those long days by the Coast Guard recognizing each of those days as one and a half."

The USCG decided that a mariner will be awarded one-and-a-half sea days for every documented twelve-hour day worked. The change to one-and-a-half sea days meant that sea time could be accumulated faster in a shorter time. The problem was everybody started doing it. The USCG had a tough time regulating who actually worked twelve-hour days and who just brought a letter for it. Most of the vessels claiming to have mariners working twelve-hour days were not inspected by the USCG, so they did not know if the vessels were legitimate or not. Consequently, the USCG no longer accepts one-and-a-half days unless well documented. Here is the Coast Guard's take on it from policy letter 09-01:

"Acceptance of Time-And-One-Half Service: With the exception of vessels in a semi-operational status, under this policy letter and vessels in reduced operating service, if a mariner works a twelve-hour day in a crew position on a vessel of over 100 gross tons, and such a work schedule is legal, time-and-one-half credit should be given. The mariner must provide adequate documentation from the operating company that the 12-hour day was authorized and practiced. Twelve-hour days will normally consist of watchstanding, but could consist of day-work directly involved with the operation and maintenance of the vessel when operating under the authority of the COI [Certificate of Inspection]. Work hours for some vessels are specified in Title 46, United States Code 8104. Sea service letters indicating possible violation of regulation or law, should be referred to a Coast Guard marine investigating officer.

Companies may apply for special consideration if their vessels have operating schedules or characteristics that they feel warrant additional service credit. Requests for such consideration may be submitted for evaluation to the National Maritime Center (NMC-4C) via the OCMI. The OCMI is the Officer in Charge of Marine Inspection for certain sectors. It is the person that is in charge of the Marine Safety Offices for the Coast Guard. The requests must include a comprehensive description of the vessel(s), operating schedule, watchstanding duties, percentage of underway service, and any other details that may support additional credit."

I included the last paragraph above from the policy letter to give mariners an avenue to defend their day-and-a-half service. If you think that the vessel you are on fits into the day-and-a-half category, and you are not receiving it, maybe your company or the vessel's owners do not know about it. Bring this to their attention and let them know they have an avenue to get approved by the NMC and USCG to issue day-and-a-half sea time. The selling point for their work is the additional mariners who will work there for the sea time. I know plenty of mariners who would work for that sea time at lower pay and harder duty. Getting sea time fast is everything when you are hawsepiping.

To ensure that your sea service qualifies for day-and-a-half, make sure it is documented properly. Many mariners will work twelve-hour days. The issue is whether it is voluntary. For example, you can work an eight-hour day on a ship for a union and then work four hours overtime, making it a twelve-hour day. However, you cannot use this scheme because the four hours extra was voluntary overtime. The USCG will not accept it as day-

and-a-half service. Use this definition above and the policy letter [09-01] to support your sea time and make sure that it is an involuntary twelve-hour day. But make sure that your sea service documentation does not exceed any legal work hours for the United States. You should be safe with twelve-hour days, but make sure the class of vessel (by the above definition and legal work limitations) is allowed to work that much.

Restricted Sea Time

Another consideration mariners must face is restricted sea time. This category is difficult if you are hawsepiping. Sometimes, due to the nature of work of a vessel, the USCG will not grant day-for-day sea time. This stipulation is something that most mariners are aware of if they have worked, or know somebody who has worked, on these types of vessels. The vessels themselves are not bad duty, and sometimes it is all you have to pick from. Just be aware of the sea time limitations and be prepared. The same policy letter [09-01] that describes day-and-a-half sea time also describes restricted sea time. It states that if a vessel is deemed to be in reduced operating status, or does not leave the dock (like a prepositioned vessel or casino vessel), one day of USCG sea time will be granted for every three days worked onboard that vessel, and a mariner can only be credited for up to 180 days of that type of sea time. If you do the math, to get 180 days of credit at three to one, a mariner would have to work 540 days (one-and-a-half years) just to get six months of sea time the USCG would recognize.

The policy letter is a bit confusing, but it helps if you treat it like an outline. For example, in reference to the numbered paragraphs like, "in accordance with paragraph 3a(2)." Find the number 3, which in this case, would be the subject at the top of the quote, "3. Regional Examination Centers (REC) shall credit such time as follows:" Go to paragraph "a. Service On Vessels That Do Not Get Underway:", then go to the subject within paragraph "a." titled "(2)- Deck department: Dockside service may be credited as follows in accordance with reference (a):" Follow to reference (a) which explains "Renewal: Service is credited as "closely related service" for renewal of licenses and MMDs. Mariners who demonstrate three years of service within the last five years, in any capacity in the deck department, will be eligible for renewal. In addition, deck officers will be required to successfully complete the Rules of the Road open-book exercise. When submitted in combination with underway service, such service may be credited at the rate of three days of service equals one day of credit up to a maximum credit of 180 days."

Here are the definitions from the policy letter [09-01]:

3. Regional Examination Centers (REC) shall credit such time as follows:

A. Service On Vessels That Do Not Get Underway: This includes vessels that are actually in operation but do not get underway (such as dockside casino vessels), and whose service is mandated by the vessel's Certificate of Inspection (COI).

i. Engineering department: Dockside service may be credited day-for-day for renewals, upgrades, recency, and original license/Merchant Mariner Document (MMD).

ii. Deck department: Dockside service may be credited as follows in accordance with reference (a):

a. Renewal: Service is credited as 'closely related service' for renewal of licenses and MMDs. Mariners who demonstrate three years of service within the last five years, in any capacity in the deck department, will be eligible for renewal. In addition, deck officers will be required to successfully complete the Rules of the Road open-book exercise. When submitted in combination with underway service, such service may be credited at the rate of three days of service equals one day of credit up to a maximum credit of 180 days.

b. Raise In Grade/Upgrade of MMD Rating: Service may be credited for upgrade if it is similar in nature to the duties performed aboard an in-service, underway vessel. Such service may be credited for up to 180 days of the service required for an upgrade at the rate of three days of service equals one day of credit.

c. Original License or MMD: Such service may be credited for up to one-half of the required service for the particular license or MMD applied for, but not more than 180 days of credit, at the rate of three days of service equals one day of credit.

B. Service Aboard Commercial Vessels That Get Underway for Only Limited Periods: This includes vessels that are actually in operation and occasionally get underway for short voyages. On any day that a vessel gets underway, service by deck and engineering crewmembers may be credited, day for day, for renewals, upgrades, recency, and original license or MMD. This recognizes crew duties necessary for preparing the vessel before and after the voyage, as well as the duties associated with even a limited period of vessel operation, which fall into regular deck and engineering responsibilities for a vessel in traditional service. On days when these vessels do not get underway, service may be credited in accordance with paragraph 3.a. (at the top of the definition)

C. Service Aboard Commercial Vessels Operating in an Artificial Impoundment: Service by deck and engineering crewmembers on vessels that are in operation within an artificial impoundment, and whose service is mandated by the COI, will be credited in accordance with paragraph 3.a. (artificial impoundment: A man-made body of water; reservoir)

D. Service Aboard Liftboats: Service may be credited without restriction on days when the vessel is underway. When elevated and in operation under authority of the vessel's

COI service may be credited as follows:

1. Engineering Department: If the engineering plant is operational and engineering personnel are standing a regular watch, then service may be credited in accordance with paragraph 3.a.

   i. If the engineering plant is non-operational, service shall be credited in the same manner as deck department personnel described in paragraph 3.a.(2).

   ii. Deck Department: When elevated for extended periods service may be credited in accordance with 3.a.(2). (3 to 1)

E. Service On Vessels In a Semi-Operational Status: This includes vessels such as oil spill response vessels, anchored (extended-period) pre-positioned ready reserve vessels, and other vessels moored and in a semi-operational or 'on-call' status, which are maintained, manned, and operated to facilitate a rapid deployment. Service may be credited without restriction on days when the vessel is underway. Moored service may be credited as follows (except as otherwise provided for in reference (b) for Military Sealift Command (MSC) operational tempo (OPTEMPO) ships and other fast sealift ships):

i. Engineering Department: If the engineering plant is operational and engineering personnel are standing a regular watch or required to perform maintenance or repair, then service may be credited in accordance with paragraph 3.a.(1). If the engineering plant is non-operational, service shall be credited in the same manner as deck department personnel described in paragraph 3.a.(2).

ii. Deck Department: When moored, service may be credited in accordance with paragraph 3.a.(2). (3 to 1)

F. Reduced Operating Service (ROS) Vessels: There are a variety of vessels that spend the majority of their time moored, with reduced crews, and limited operating systems. Service may be credited without restriction on days when the vessel is underway. During all other times service shall be credited as follows:

i. Engineering Department: Service shall be credited in accordance with reference (c).

ii. Deck Department: Service shall be credited in accordance with paragraph 3.a.(2).

G. Oil Spill Response Barges (OSRBs): These vessels are non-self propelled and spend significant time at anchor. They are not required to have licensed personnel onboard and do not have a pilothouse or engineering space. Service may be credited as follows:

i. While engaged in spill response operations or exercises, regardless of underway, anchored, or moored status, service may be credited day-for-day toward deck department ratings and renewals.

ii. While anchored or moored in a standby status, service may be credited at the rate of one day sea service credit for every four days worked toward deck department ratings and renewals for up to six months of the service required for any deck rating that requires 12 months or more of service, and not more than half of the service required for other deck ratings (i.e., AB-OSV & AB-Fish). Such service may also be credited as 'closely related service' for the purpose of renewing a deck rating.

iii. While engaged in oil collection or transfer operations, service may be credited day-for-day toward qualification as Tankerman-PIC (Barge). While anchored or moored and in a standby status, such service may be credited as meeting the requirements contained in 46 CFR 13.303(a)(2).

iv. (Service on OSRBs will not be credited toward qualification as Rating Forming Part of the Navigation Watch under reference (b)."

All policy letters, CFRs, and legal matters are always written in paragraph outline form to save space and prevent writing the same things over and over. It is a game of paragraph "referencing."

It takes practice to read and understand policies, but it is a skill you have to master if you want a better chance at taking tests and understanding the laws on which the maritime industry is based. You will be a better mariner and ahead of the game if you understand the rules. The captains, mates, and mariners I have worked with and respected the most, have had a competent understanding of the CFRs and USCG policies regarding their job. It is a very useful tool that takes out any guesswork and interpretation.

Other Ways to Get Sea Time

Now that we know how much time you need for everything, and how the USCG views sea time, some final additions to the sea time matrix need to be explained. There are other ways to acquire sea time other than being on deck onboard a vessel. This is taken from policy letter [10-01] regarding time spent in USCG-approved classes that count for sea time:

Applying Credit For Course Completion In Lieu Of Sea Service

1. GENERAL. Sea service credit acquired through completion of an approved course may be accepted as set forth in this enclosure. In each evaluation of sea service credit applied to a transaction affecting a credential subject to the STCW, the basic rule is that the STCW's sea service requirements must be met

through actual sea service. Once this rule is met, sea service credit granted for course completion may be accepted to meet any domestic requirements that exceed the STCW's standards. With the exception of the requirement for conformity with the STCW's requirements, the standards listed below do not apply to the approved training programs conducted on nautical schoolships or at the maritime academies.

2. DECK LICENSES AND QUALIFIED RATINGS.

   A. LICENSES. Course completion may substitute for up to eight-months sea-service credit required for a raise in grade from third mate to second mate. The applicant will already have met the STCW's sea-service requirements for certification at the officer-in-charge level when he or she first applied for initial certification as third mate or third assistant engineer. Applicants who use courses-in-lieu of-sea-service credit to apply for the second mate's license may find themselves short of the required, total amount of sea service when they ultimately apply for a master's certification.

   [Author's Note: An example of this type of class is 'Advanced Shiphandling for Third Mates.' It is a ten-day class and is approved by the Coast Guard to count for sixty days sea time toward a second mate's license. Ask your schools about classes like these. They are rare, but they exist.]

   B. QUALIFIED RATINGS. For initial issuance of an able seaman endorsement, the maximum limits for substitution of course completion for sea service are listed below. The mariner must have had actual sea service to qualify for the STCW's proficiencies, rating forming part of a navigational watch and proficient in survival craft, which are both pre-requisites for qualification as an able seaman.:

   i. Able seaman-unlimited—12-months sea-service credit may be accepted;

   ii. Able seaman-limited—6-months sea-service credit may be accepted;

   iii. Able seaman-special—4-months sea-service credit may be accepted;

   C. To raise the level of certification as an able seaman, up to one-third of the additional sea service required by the upgrade may consist of sea-service credit granted for completion of another relevant approved course(s).

Coast Guard-approved classes for sea-service credit are a great way to make up short periods of sea time. If you are short a certain number of days and do not want to sign on another ship for a four-month tour or wait around for that perfect thirty-day relief job to come up (like everybody else is waiting for), look into taking a class for that sea time. It is a good way to do it. The classes cost money, but you can see if your union or company will reimburse you for them. Always try to get reimbursement. Any USCG-approved course is essential to your job and should be reimbursed. If not, it can be a tax write off for work purposes. So what if it also helped you go from third mate to second mate? That is just an added bonus.

Be aware that the policy letter states the limits on how much approved course time you can substitute for real sea time for deck licenses and AB time. It also states, and this is important, that you might be short on time when you look to upgrade again. For example, let's take the incident of using the Advanced Shiphandling class for sixty days' sea time to upgrade from third mate to second mate. The USCG is saying when it is time for you to apply for your chief mate/master license, that sixty days you used to get to second mate from third mate via the shiphandling course *cannot* be used to upgrade to chief mate. You will have to make up the time as a second mate, meaning you will have to sail sixty extra days to fulfill the entire sea time requirement. The way the USCG has the deck licensing set up now, the real jumps are from AB to third mate and second mate to chief mate. Third to second and chief mate to master is only a matter of sea time. They are saying they would rather you use those approved courses in lieu of sea time for the easy upgrades from third to second and chief mate to master. You have already tested for the higher license under the new scheme anyway. The Coast Guard does not mind if you take a class or two to make up that sea time as quickly as possible. The way I see it, it is a promotion based purely on time. You can work as quickly as possible to get it. The classes sometimes help if you are looking to get the upgrade quickly. As a hawsepiper, you might have some random college classes that could transfer as sea time. Usually they don't, but it doesn't hurt to ask the REC.

Another way to get sea time is by teaching a class. This time also can be used for that easy upgrade, but not for the big one from second to chief mate or AB to third mate. The CFR states that two days of instructing at a USCG-approved institution is worth one day of sea time at your current license (46CFR10.211). You may only use up to six months of that sea time (one year of teaching) toward the upgrade.

Other sea-related jobs, like port engineer or captain of the port, allow for sea time under 46CFR10.211, but not all of them are two for one. Port engineer and shipyard superintendent count as three for one with a maximum of six months. 46CFR10.211 details other sea time equivalents, so read it carefully. The main point is you need to be proactive on sea time. Make sure you are informed as much as the USCG regarding your sea time. You do not want to be the one who applies for a license, MMD, or upgrade, only to find out you do not have enough time. Obviously, the best method is to actually get underway, but be aware and knowledgeable of all the ways to get sea time.

As you climb the licensing ladder, the USCG has printed documents that illustrate additional ways to get the upgrades in the sea time you need. For example, we read that if you are a third mate sailing as an AB, your sea time will count toward your second mate licenses on a two-for-one basis, but only up to six months can be used.

The sea time requirements for each license are in the USCG applications themselves. Read them carefully because they include particulars about each license or MMD regarding how many days you need aboard select tonnages and in what ratings you need to be working. As we saw before, a third mate's license requires 1,080 days of sea time total. At least eighteen months of that sea time is required to be on vessels 1,600 GT or above. The other 540 days can be on vessels 200 GT or above. Also, 180 days of that sea time has to be in the capacity of a watchstanding AB.

If any sea time does not fit into any category, call, e-mail, or visit the REC. It is always a good idea to find out exactly what you need. The REC has everything documented and can guide you to where you need to go. If you find you are not getting the answers you need, go to the USCG Web site. You also can e-mail any questions to me at www.thenewhawsepipe.com. I will try my best to solve the problem.

Engineering Time for Deck and Vice Versa

The final sea time option I want to discuss is time spent in a different department onboard a vessel counting for sea time in another department. This is usually for folks who have tried different departments first to see where they want to work.

Unlimited class vessels usually have three departments, Deck, Engineering, and Steward. The ship has to look good and not hit anything, the engines have to run and be maintained, and people have to eat. The Coast Guard views some of the time spent in each department as credible, although usually it is deck and engineering that they recognize. Stewarding, or basically the food department, is not outlined as counting toward deck or engineering licenses. It is in a category of its own.

You can apply a maximum of three months' experience in the engine room on a vessel of appropriate tonnage toward a deck license, and vice versa. It is not a lot, but it is something.

Like we saw before, each deck or engineering license has its specific requirements, which makes obtaining them extremely confusing. All the sea time requirements are listed in the 46CFR, part 10, which is entitled "Licensing of Maritime Personnel" and 46CFR part 12 "Certification of Seaman."

Recency

Recency is a pesky little thing the USCG requires of each mariner getting an MMD, upgrade, or increase in scope (Inland to Near Coastal or Oceans for example). It is the process of keeping your sea time current in the industry. Because sea time never expires, the USCG requires you to have been recently active in the maritime industry. The recency requirement is not all that stringent, but it is still required. Do not overlook it.

Those who sail regularly will not have to deal with recency. The USCG will automatically look at your sea time and check for recency. The folks who have to watch out are the part timers, mariners who have gone on to try something else and then returned to the maritime industry, or just want to keep their license going though they are no longer sailing.

Because sea time does not expire, mariners can get the required time needed for an upgrade in license and then stop shipping altogether for a long period. When they feel like coming back, they can apply for that upgrade without having been to sea for awhile.

To remedy this problem, recency came into play. Recency usually is the easiest requirement to fulfill, but be mindful of it. The USCG will ask you for proof of recency, and you had better be ready to give it to them. The official definition from the Coast Guard application is as follows:

> "The applicant for any original license, endorsement, or raise-of-grade of license must have at least 90 days of qualifying service on vessels of appropriate tonnage or horsepower within the three years immediately preceding the date of application."

Many different forms of sea time can suffice for recency. Each avenue of sea time, be it restricted, instructing, simulator, or any other form of sea time discussed, usually can be counted for recency. Talk to the REC to make sure you have the qualified sea time for recency. If you do not use your license or document, but want to keep it current, contact the USCG and tell them what you want to do *before the license expires!*

If you have not used your license, you may take an open book exam to keep it current. Other ways are to take a CG-approved refresher course or pass the refresher exam for each particular license. (This is taken directly from the USCG Web site.)

When renewing a license or MMD, other than an upgrade, make sure that you know how much sea time you need and which is applicable. You do not want to go to the USCG to renew only to find that some of your sea time does not count. Talk to USCG and ask them specifically what sea time will count, and get the recency so you know you have it.

Renewals

You can apply for a renewal before your present documentation or license expires. Be ahead of the game. You must always keep a close eye on the expirations for all documents. One of the check lists before you decide to start looking for a ship is to spread out all your certificates and documents and see what needs renewing. Government endorsements like "small arms" are good for only one year and need constant attention. I have seen mariners, including me, refused jobs because they had certificates or documents that were expired. One time I was in New Orleans, waiting for a job on a government vessel. I was an applicant for MMP at the time and had a pretty old shipping card. Only one guy had an older card than mine, and his was almost a year old. No one had a better card than this guy. When the job came up for two third mates, about five of us threw in for it. The guy with the old card and I got the two third mate jobs.

While reviewing the documents and certifications, the union patrolman noticed that the guy's FCC Global Marine Distress and Safety System (GMDSS) certificate was about to expire. He refused the man the job right then and there. The guy was furious. The certificate was current at the time, but would have expired during the 120-day contract. The agreement with this shipping company was that all certificates had to be valid for the duration of the contract or the employee would be refused the job. This guy had flown up from Hawaii, only to be denied the job and made to watch as much newer mates got it. He had blown all his travel expenses and a $40,000 to $50,000 four-month job because of an expired certificate. I have seen it more than once. Make sure all certificates are current before you do anything. Renew what needs to be renewed in a timely fashion.

Chapter Four
Classes, Endorsements, and Schools

This chapter includes a list and description of every class needed to get the STCW 95 *Officer in Charge of a Navigational Watch.* Mariners that qualify for any deck license or MMD (OS or AB) must also satisfy the STCW 95 requirements by taking the prescribed classes relating to each license or MMD.

This chapter also details endorsements that can be added to your STCW 95 document and additional union or company requirements. This means some classes are required for the specific license, some are required for specific companies or ships. All of it means that mariners never stop having to obtain additional endorsements and certificates.

To help put the ball back in your court on USCG-approved schools offering these classes, I will guide you through the CG Web site to show you which schools are really approved. This transfer of power is nice for the mariner, because you have a system of checks and balances for every class and endorsement certificate. They are all listed on the CG Web site.

Some schools say they are approved, but are not really recognized by the USCG. These schools usually charge considerably less for their classes. Stick to the USCG list on the Web site. Go to the USCG Home Page at http://www.uscg.mil/stcw/ and click on "Merchant Mariner Info Center" on the left-hand side. Scroll down to "Approved Courses" and click on it. This will provide a list of all the classes and subjects. Click on any of the subjects or programs, and a list of all the approved schools will come up for that subject or program. The list will also include contact information for the schools, and describe what the school is approved to do for that subject (i.e., are they allowed to sign assessments in the classroom). These school lists are posted as PDF files, so make sure your computer has Adobe Reader. This is an essential Web site when looking for schools. Anybody can say anything about their classes, but this site lists the official USCG-approved schools and classes. Check it out before you sign up. Ask the school if it satisfies the STCW requirements for Officer in Charge of a Navigational Watch and if any assessments can be signed (which I will cover in the next chapter) in that class. When I first started doing this, none of the schools were approved to sign any assessments in class. Now, almost every maritime school is approved to sign assessments in the classroom, which is a big help to the mariner. It gives you a choice to get them signed in class or on a ship. Go to each school's approval page and double check for each assessment and class for which they are approved.

It takes the NMC a while to get the official approval back to the school. If you take the class before it is approved, the USCG might not accept it and you have wasted your money. Following the list on the Web site will eliminate this problem. The schools know about this Web site, but a lot of mariners do not. The schools have become much better now with classes, assessments, and approvals, so you really should not have any problems at any school. If you do, let the Coast Guard know about it. The school's livelihood depends on the students.

To get to AB, you need to take the STCW Basic Safety Training, which consists of four modules. The first is Proficiency in Survival Craft, which means you will get wet. You must perform duties in a simulated life raft situation, usually in a nice warm pool and not the Bering Sea in the winter. You must get in the pool, swim around, put on a survival suit (not necessarily in that order), and get yourself into the floating life raft. You must practice righting an overturned life raft in the water and other duties in and out of the water. The second module, First Aid, deals with identification of different bone breaks, bandaging, splinting, and other basic first aid tasks. The Social Responsibility module includes schooling in the proper etiquette onboard coed vessels and how to behave in a professional manner. Basic Firefighting teaches mariners how to deal with different types of fires, use various firefighting techniques and extinguishing agents and use protective firefighting equipment, including instruction on being part of a fire team. BST usually lasts one week total and costs approximately $800. Costs vary by school. Check the school approval list on the Web site for BST and start calling.

Life Boatman is another requirement for every mariner to have, AB and above. It usually is a four-day class that covers the theory, policies, requirements of lifeboats aboard vessels, practical demonstrations in raising and lowering a lifeboat, competency in oar commands, and lifeboat navigation and piloting. The cost for this course averages $500. Again, each school's prices will be different, but $500 is a good figure to budget for this course. The test consists of seventy-five questions, multiple choice, with a passing grade of 70 percent and a practical demonstration of oar commands, lowering and raising the lifeboat, and being the lifeboat coxswain. The certificate is good for one year for submission to the USCG.

AB is a class that can be anywhere from three days to three weeks. The AB exam covers many subjects. Navigation, line handling, knot tying, running rigging (all moving parts on the deck, name and purpose), and safety nomenclature are just some of the subjects covered in AB class. Also, a practical demonstration of tying ten knots and either one back splice or eye splice is required. This is also a test that can be taken at a school's location, and the certificate can be submitted to the Coast Guard for up to one year. Meaning it does not have to be turned into the Coast Guard right away. Make sure you get all the certificates you need before submitting them to the Coast Guard.

Every time the USCG changes or updates your document, it charges a fee. To minimize this fee, submit all documents and certificates at the same time.

For every mate's license that is oceangoing more than 500 tons, you must take a program of classes called Officer in Charge of a Navigational Watch. If you need the Officer in Charge of a Navigational Watch STCW certificate for your license, these are the classes you will need, and I have listed them in the order in which I think you should take them. Every school is different, and they might already have a schedule that you have to follow. Also, each school differs in pricing. It varies all over the country, so be sure to shop around.

Radar Observer usually is a five-day course required for all licenses 500 tons and above, Inland to Oceans. It introduces radar as a navigational tool and covers its purpose, reason for invention, and how it works. Students should learn the basics of radar interpretation, piloting and navigation, radar weaknesses and errors, plotting basic collision avoidance on maneuvering boards, using radar bearings and ranges from navigation, and understanding relative motion vs. true motion. The class should consist of a lot of hands-on plotting, different collision configurations to really drive home the use of radar, and how to use all controls of the radar. This certificate needs to be renewed every five years along with your license and SCTW certificate. The cost is usually around $500.

Automatic Radar Plotting Aids (ARPA) is the advanced version of Radar Observer. I recommend taking them together because the basics of the radar will still be fresh in your head. Some schools have prerequisite classes before taking others. I took my ARPA class at Piney Point, Maryland, in the SIU school. That school required mariners to have Bridge Resource Management and Radar Observer before taking ARPA. Each school has its own program of which classes they require as prerequisites. Make sure you look into each school you are thinking of attending and ask if the classes have prerequisites.

ARPA is a five-day class about all functions and theory of an ARPA system, how to use it for acquiring targets, collision avoidance, ARPA weaknesses and error identification, additional navigational tools, and much more. The class has a lot of hands-on practice with different types of ARPAs, and should be approved to sign all ARPA and radar assessments after successful completion.

Bridge Resource Management (BRM) is a class designed to create teamwork on the bridge and educate deck officers in the resources available, human and electronic, and how to use them. It can be three to five days long and incorporate everything from voyage planning and presentation to simulator drills on communication and bridge team execution and the history of marine accidents due to error chains.

This class, for most schools now, is coupled with another class called Watchkeeping. The two are closely related and usually take ten days total for both classes.

Watchkeeping focuses on bridge watchstanding procedures for deck officers. Incorporated into the class should be rules of the road; keeping a safe navigational watch while underway, at anchor, and in port; log keeping; resource management; and maybe some simulator time. Though the class usually is ten days, this present a potential problem. BRM is a class that has been required for some time, but Watchkeeping is fairly new. The problem is that some mariners have already taken BRM and only need Watchkeeping. If you fall into this category, find a school that has been approved to offer the classes separately. If you have not taken either class, then this will not matter, you can take it anywhere.

I already had BRM under my belt from another school before taking Watchkeeping. I went to two or three schools to see if I could take just the Watchkeeping portion of the class. Some schools said no. They had been approved by the USCG and NMC to teach the classes together and could not separate them. They were tailoring the classes to folks who needed all the classes and not to someone like me who had some of them already. I finally found a school that had been approved to teach them separately, even though they were scheduled together.

If you have some classes already and are not going to the same school for everything, shop around because each school has its own rules and schedules. Some are strict with their rules. Others will work with you to get the classes you need in the time frame you need them.

Basic and Advanced Firefighting is another combination of two classes in one. Basic Firefighting is a module in your BST, as outlined earlier, and you should be able to use the certificate in conjunction with Advanced Firefighting. This means that if you took BST, which includes Basic Firefighting, within six months of having to take Advanced Firefighting, you should have to take only the advanced portion of the class. Usually this is not the case, because you take BST to get your AB, then it is well past six months before you take Advanced Firefighting for your license, so you just redo both for the total five days. These configurations are rare, but keep it in mind if you are taking BST and then Advanced Firefighting close together you might not have to take Basic Firefighting again. This configuration is up to the schools and how they got their classes approved by the USCG. (Again, it is advisable to check the approval Web site). This list is subject to change. One school might say they will give you up to a year for your BST certificates, another school might say only three months. Regardless of the time, they are only doing it so the information is still fresh in your head from basic to advanced. Firefighting, in my opinion, is the most physically strenuous and taxing class you will take. I have seen guys in good shape drop like flies in the intense heat and blinding smoke and flames, which only makes matters worse. My advice is keep calm, make sure you have your fire equipment on correctly, follow the instructor's procedure, and you will emerge with a certificate.

Since basic has been discussed, advanced is an obvious elaboration on the training and use of fire equipment and extinguishing agents, including lifesaving and more intense drills. Some schools have your fire team make up a scenario and lead the class through the whole thing in the fire simulator. It develops teamwork and efficiency. It also gives mariners a good look at how hot, dangerous, and miserable a fire onboard can be.

Coastal and Terrestrial Navigation is a class I recommend before Celestial Navigation. It gives mariners a basic view on charting and using plotting tools. This is important for Celestial. Even if you reduce your celestial sights right, you still have to plot them correctly or you will miss the entire problem on the test. Coastal and Terrestrial is another combination class that usually lasts ten days, a week of each. It focuses on all the traditional aspects of navigation, like using visual bearings and radar ranges to plot fixes, bow/beam bearings, and how to actually plot on a chart and maintain an active navigational plot with frequent fix intervals. It also includes compass correction by taking azimuth and amplitudes, which are visual bearings taken of celestial bodies. All modes of sailings, which are mathematically determining courses and distances via formulas, are included. There are obviously more subjects, but these are an idea of where your head needs to be when you enter those classes.

Celestial Navigation is a course designed to cover the basics of fixing the ship's position by celestial bodies; by far the coolest part of navigation. Although it is a lost art, celestial navigation is still a vital part of being at sea. The history of celestial navigation and the drive of humans to figure out how to do it are simply amazing. It is what made our job possible in the first place, especially global transits. Unfortunately, celestial navigation has been reduced to a couple of azimuths a day and that is just plugged into a computer for gyro error. Full celestial days are rarely practiced anymore except for military training. Celestial Navigation is a required class, and if you want to know more about a subject than the other guy, this is the subject to learn and practice. The USCG and IMO require all means of navigation to be used onboard as a prudent rule. Celestial navigation obviously is part of that. You will be happy if you really take to it and find yourself in a lifeboat one day. Not a bad talent to possess. Don't forget the sextant.

Celestial Navigation can be from one week to one month long. It covers all facets of the subject, from the history to present day applications. It should cover all tools and publications required and how each problem is reduced. Practical applications include solving for rising and setting of celestial bodies; local apparent noon; amplitudes; azimuths; lines of position from the sun, moon, planets and stars; running fixes; and more. There should also be practical application on the use and correction of the marine sextant and chronometer. The test I took for this class was only ten questions, and to pass you could miss only two. It is a hard class, with a lot of math, but, again, it is totally conquerable. If you struggle with math, or are just not getting the celestial system, I recommend meeting with fellow classmates after class to go over the concepts and problems covered. We did that when I took it and everyone passed, even the guys who didn't think they had a chance. With practice (and a lot of it) celestial can be such a fulfilling craft to master.

If you really have trouble with math or navigation concepts, don't fret. You can take basic navigation and math prep classes before taking any of these STCW-required classes. If you have any doubts, take a prep class before the SCTW class. The schools understand that these classes are not easy. Some of the schools have tried to solve that problem by offering non-STCW beginning classes to prepare the student for basic navigation, marine math, and other subjects. They are extremely helpful to students and improve their skills and their passing grades. Ask the schools what they offer regarding some math prep classes.

Emergency Procedures and Search and Rescue usually are another combination class. Emergency Procedures averages three days. Search and Rescue is two days. Most schools combine these into one week of class or more.

Emergency procedures touch on what to do when things do not go well onboard ship. It focuses on collisions, groundings, passenger and crew emergencies, fire/explosions, loss of power, steering, and other emergencies. The class focuses on procedures and regulations of which an officer should be aware from the beginning of an emergency until the end, including the paperwork and salvage/repair of the ships after a serious marine incident.

Search and Rescue teaches you how to participate in a search and rescue mission as a merchant marine officer.

To prepare you in the event of a search and rescue mission, this class goes through the procedures that a merchant vessel would follow in a search and rescue operation. These include your vessel assuming on-scene command, conducting search and rescue patterns (expanding square and vector searches), contacting the proper authorities worldwide, and more. If the class is more in-depth at each particular school, you might visit a Coast Guard small boat station or be visited by Coast Guard personnel.

GMDSS is required for any person assigned to operate GMDSS equipment onboard a vessel (if the ship has it, you need the certificate). This class usually is two weeks long, but can be longer. I had an excellent teacher, so I loved the class, but to most folks this is a killer. Two tests are given at the end; one is one hundred questions, which gives you your STCW certificate; the other is twenty-five questions and gives you your Federal Communications Commission (FCC) marine radio operator's permit. The FCC license has a five-year expiration date, and I have seen a mate lose a job because his FCC license expired. You know how I feel about expired certificates and licenses.

GMDSS should take you through the history of radio and communications. It should outline and discuss the emergency equipment and how each piece works and the publications and documentation regarding GMDSS and how to operate it. All the frequencies, including MF/HF, VHF DSC, telex, International Marine Maritime Satellite (INMARSAT), and more should be explained and operated via simulator or low power vessel equipment (as to not bother actual ships in the harbor). GMDSS basically deals with all the communications onboard a vessel and how to operate them. Assessments need to be completed on simulated or real equipment, and the written test requires a lot of frequency memorization. It is a passable class, but it is not easy. It does get a bit dry at times, and the GMDSS console onboard vessels, unfortunately, do not get used that much anymore, but do not be one of those mates who do not know how to operate it correctly!

Electronic Navigation is a week-long class that studies the electronics on the bridge by which to navigate. This was a weird class for me because I thought we would be studying at the Global Positioning System (GPS), since that is the main piece of electronic navigation on the bridge today. I was wrong. In my electronic navigation class, we studied: LORAN (Long Range Navigation), Automatic Identification System (AIS), and Electronic Chart Display and Information System (ECDIS). I was surprised that we only briefly discussed the GPS. I asked the instructor why, and he said, "LORAN is a dying, but interesting concept, and I feel it is important to know in regards to the history of electronic navigation. AIS and ECDIS are tools that are onboard ships and no one has any training in, and need the most emphasis today." GPS needs less instruction because it is so widely used. You obviously will touch on more subjects than these, but ECDIS, AIS, and GPS should be the main ones. In my class we also touched on the history of electronic navigation, including Optimized Method for Estimated Guidance Accuracy VLF Navigation System (Omega), LORAN, and GPS. We had laptop computers and followed along with the instructor as we looked at baud rates and how the interface happens with all the converging electronic systems and practiced all applications of AIS and ECDIS, including chart corrections, chart selection, sending and receiving messages, route planning and actively maintaining an ECDIS and AIS plot reviewing all the options and tools available.

This class is an eye-opener to the "new" bridge. All the electronics are digital and can talk to each other. As a merchant officer, it is your responsibility to understand how they work and use all equipment efficiently. The biggest problem out there today is that mariners sometimes only learn a piece of equipment when they really need it. It is a dangerous game. You do not want to be learning something when it is time to already know it, like a traffic situation or pilotage waters. Learn your equipment in advance. A class like electronic navigation will help you understand it better.

Basic Meteorology was one of my favorite five-day classes. I came into it thinking it was going to be a snooze, but was surprised at how interesting it was. As I always say, every school is different, but the basics of the class should be how our weather works on this planet. High and low pressure systems, wind, currents, clouds (height and types), fog, sea-state, tracking bad weather, dewpoint, humidity, fronts, weather information, and where to find it. These are all subjects that should be in the class.

Most of it was classroom for me, but in your class you might take a walk outside and take some meteorological observations and make predictions. The class puts into perspective how the weather and our oceans interact with each other to make it a good day or a bad day upon the high seas. Let's face it, we can't all be that old salt that when his left knee starts hurting he'll grunt, "Storm's a comin'!"

Ship's Construction and Stability is a difficult class, and is usually five days long. I say this to warn mariners about the stability formulas. The "ship's construction" part is not so bad. The general identification of all the plating and framing of a ship and how the design and engineering goes into the hull shape for purpose and efficiency should be some subjects covered. The stability formulas are a pain because there are a lot of them. The even bigger pain is the formulas are not allowed in the Coast Guard testing room, meaning you must memorize them. The good side is that the USCG Deck Safety test usually does not have a lot of stability questions. The test at the end of this class obviously has a lot of them, so during the five-day class mariners should do plenty of different stability problems. My advice is: practice. Do as many stability problems as you can during the five days. It is imperative that you understand the basics of stability for your job; like the difference between a "stiff" and "tender" vessel, a vessel's righting arm and how to change it, negative stability and the mathematical and visual signs of a vessel heading in that direction, how a vessel's center of gravity moves, and what factors affect it. A mariner should know the definition of each letter or letters in stability formulas (G, M, GM, Z, K, etc.) and how each can be manipulated. In regards to the numbers and the tests, my philosophy is that a third mate should know where to find the stability formulas onboard ship, but to memorize them is not necessary except for the Coast Guard test. A competent understanding of how the vessel moves on the water regarding stability and how the vessel's righting arm works would be good enough as a third mate. There are a lot of factors regarding ship's stability, and it is constantly changing due to the dynamics of buoyancy and gravity on the water. It is a tough subject to get your head around, but don't worry, start at the beginning and practice!

Cargo Handling and Storage is a class I recommend taking with Ship's Construction and Stability. I think they go together at most schools, but the schedule may differ. This week-long class details all the methods of loading and storing different cargoes: bagged, palleted, bulk, liquid, container, and vapor. It should describe all stowing methods, dating back to the early shipping days. The class also should cover different loading and unloading equipment like cranes, hoses, belts, and the "Safe Working Load," and signs of stress on each kind.

Basic Shiphandling usually is a combination class. Another required small class is Steering Control. This course usually is tucked in with Shiphandling. Make sure that it is when you go to this class. Ask the school and make sure it is on your certificate at the end of the five days (usually a five-day total course for both). If Steering Control is not, ask where it is in the course scheme. I have yet to see it offered individually from any school, but that does not mean that it won't be.

Shiphandling usually is a simulator class, or they may use scaled ship models that you can drive around or control. Either way, it is a fun and educational class. It should cover the general maneuverability of vessels through the water, stopping distances, slowing down, speeding up, docking and undocking, turning circles, advance and transfer, shallow vs. deep water maneuverability, deep vs. shallow draft, moments of force, squat, effects of wind and current, and more. All of this should be demonstrated with a simulator or ship models. When I went to this class, it had only two students and it was the first time it was taught. It was in a simulator and the other student and I had a great time because we got so much time conning. I remember taking a container ship out of Barber's Cut in the Houston ship channel without tugs or help. It was a really great experience because you get to do things normally out of context in our profession. Mariners should see how a vessel handles in an emergency. When the inevitable happens, there actually is a right and wrong way to crash, and this class is a perfect forum in which to practice.

Gyro and Magnetic Compasses probably should be one of the classes an AB can come in with some experience from standing helm watches. This is usually a three-day course and explains everything about the electronic gyro compass and magnetic compass. The important thing is how they work. Everybody uses them, but not everyone knows how the gyro can stay on true north all the time and how it gets its errors. The magnetic compass, to me, is fascinating. The subject of the earth's magnetism can get a little deep, but it is good stuff. In the class you should be able to look at the inner workings of these two compasses and get to move some magnets around to try to "swing" the compass. Onboard vessels, they usually farm that out to contractors specialized in that field, so this might be the only time you get to do it or see it done. We used to do it ourselves in the Coast Guard, but not anymore. If contractors manage this on your vessel, watch how they do it. It is good knowledge to have.

Medical Care Provider takes first aid to the next level working on the assumption that, as first responder, you are the first called in a medical emergency. It should take you through checking the pulse, blood pressure, and respiratory signs, and making observations based on that information. It should explain what standard questions to ask to get the most information the quickest from a victim or patient. It also should provide education on medical communications at sea and how to initiate these. The course also might include brief discussions on medicine and diseases and managing both. This satisfies your CPR and First Aid cards, which are required by the Coast Guard. An additional subject to CPR is Automated External Defibrillators (AEDs). These electronic machines are easy to use and should be explained and demonstrated in this class. The USCG and Occupational Safety and Health Administration (OSHA) require AEDs to be onboard U.S.-flagged vessels. Make sure you know how to use one. This class is required to get to third mate. It is a week long and can be coupled with Medical Person in Charge (MED PIC), which totals a ten-day course. Medical Care Provider is a prerequisite for MED PIC, but the two-week MED PIC includes Medical Care Provider (week one). This is good because if you already have taken Medical Care Provider you might only have to take the last week of MED PIC to get the certificate, or you can take MED PIC. My advice is to take them both at the same time. This way you will have no problem with any time gaps.

Flashing Light or Visual Communications is required by mariners wanting the scope of oceans on their license. If you have a limited scope like near coastal, you must complete this course to get the oceans endorsement. Some schools have a class for this, others provide only a self-study via computer programs, or a flashing light itself. In my opinion, the test is the most intense two minutes of your life. If you have ever sat and stared at a flashing light and tried to decode it, you know what I am talking about. The most important thing about flashing light is the fact that it is coded. The message traffic sent are letters and numbers representing something. For example, you will see the letters D and E flashed in succession and so quickly that it almost looks like something else. Do not be fooled. DE is a code for "transmission to follow." It is merely a prompt for the actual message. It can look like Morse B.

Even though it is a short test, it is not easy. I recommend learning Morse Code by writing it, saying it, and watching it. Then start to decode letters that you see everyday, like a stop sign or advertisements. Break every word you see into Morse Code. That will prepare you for the test. There are also great computer programs at school that let you take practice tests and more. Get to know the format in which the messages are sent, as they are all in code. You can study it other ways, this is just what worked for me. The test consists of two or three different things. First, you should have to identify some call signs and coded information. This should be to track your competency in decoding. Second, the letters and numbers come in another code, which has to be recorded, then translated out of a publication called "HO201 International Code of Signals," so not only do you have to get the flashing light right, you have to get the translation in the book right.

Two other classes from the policy letter [01-02] are needed. They are Life Saving and Prevention of Pollution of the Marine Environment. These classes are bundled into other classes, so you will not see these offered separately. As long as you complete the program of classes, Lifesaving and Prevention of Pollution of the Marine Environment are included.

Take these classes one at a time. This is a long list of subjects, but set yourself realistic goals. Balance your life, talk to your kids and spouse, and explain what this kind of sacrifice means. Remember, this will not work without a plan.

Chief Mate/Master

After you have obtained the third/second mate license and have worked up the sea time to upgrade to second mate, you should look to the next stage of classes, assessments, and sea time for chief mate/master. Figuring out what you need to do will be much easier now that you have established yourself within the industry. Most of the required courses are merely advanced courses in the same subjects as third/second mate, but look at Coast Guard Policy Letter [04-02] on the USCG Web site, which lists all the courses needed for the upgrade (plus the assessments in chapter six). The list of classes is as follows: Advanced Navigation, Meteorology, COLREGS, Stability, Shiphandling Search and Rescue, Radar, ARPA, Marine Propulsion Plants, Ship Management including Emergency Response and Cargo Handling. Most schools have an upgrade program for chief mate/master with all the courses. Some of these classes are satisfied, like Search and Rescue Radar and ARPA, through the third/second mate program. I list them all to make sure you are prepared. Radar has to be renewed every five years, so make sure you are current. I also list all the classes because some second mates have had their license before the new rules came into effect, and have never taken any of the new classes. If you have questions, consult the REC and Policy Letter [04-02]. A second mate should know what is needed for advancement and where to find it. I still run into second mates who do not know where the assessments are on the Web site. As a general guide, make sure the chief mate/master courses correspond to the practical assessments. There are fifty-three assessments for chief/mate master and the control numbers are [M-1-1A] to [M-9-1D] The assessments also can be signed onboard, which a lot of second mates do. Practical assessments are covered in greater detail in chapter six.

Endorsements

Endorsements are the long list of additional certificates and requirements set forth by company, union, or vessel. For example, if you are interested in joining Military Sealift Command (MSC) or other Military Sealift Command vessels as an officer or unlicensed crewmember, certain additional requirements must be met. To sign onto an MSC vessel, the vessel might require the individual to have endorsements in damage control, government vessel familiarization, small arms training, explosive cargo handling, forklift operator's licenses, force protection and vessel security.

These are separate classes held just for the different MSC vessels. Other commercial vessels might require you have small arms and vessel security officer training too. Another example is tankerman PIC for officers and tanker assistant for the unlicensed crewmember to work on tank vessels or tank barges.

Be well versed in all endorsements needed to sail on the vessels of your choice. The problem is the list of endorsements and certificates never stops growing, and companies are always changing their requirements. One of the big certificates in question today is vessel security. Before September 11th, it was not as imperative for officers to have the vessel security course. As the Department of Homeland Security, which now houses the USCG, focuses on improving security onboard vessels, new requirements must be met. The mariner's responsibility in this situation is to be proactive. Talk to the company, union, or vessel to see what additional classes, certificates or endorsements are needed, and what are some of the future concerns. What else will be required a year from now? What should you be working on to be ahead of the game?

Another topic regarding these additional requirements is whether they are USCG-approved courses. The ship security officer course was only recently approved by the USCG. When that happens to a course, certain guidelines must be met. A test must be given at the end of the course, and evaluations of the course, school, and instructor must be given to the students to fill out. It is important to know which are USCG-approved and which are merely additional classes required by the companies or unions.

For example, some companies require the officers to be proficient in computers, and the union that you work for will offer a computer course if you do not have that experience. Another would be a diesel endorsement for deck officers working on diesel-powered vessels. This is a course that familiarizes a deck officer with the throttles or engine order telegraph (EOT) of the ship: How to change from bridge to engine room control, test the engine EOT response, bring a vessel up to speed, and reduce speed using the throttles. These are not USCG-approved courses, but they are required by some companies before you can sail on their vessels. When I joined MMP as a third mate, I had all my licenses and certificates and was eager for a job. I signed up, only to find I could not sail on any of the container ships because I did not have certain certificates the shipping companies required. I was not too happy about it, but learned a valuable lesson. Know what you need before you need it. If you are thinking about shipping with a union, talk to the folks at the union halls and ask them about additional requirements for each shipping company. MMP, for example, has a nice handout in its welcome package that included a matrix of all their companies and what each required in addition to the license and STCW.

The final item to explain about non-USCG-approved certificates is equivalency. Equivalency is a tool a mariner can use to qualify for certificates without taking the classes. For example, the diesel endorsement I needed for the container ship companies was a hard class to get because it was rarely offered. In lieu of the class, I could ship on another diesel class ship that did not require the certificate (another company obviously, but still with the same union). If I was an officer onboard for ninety days or more, that satisfied the diesel class and I had my endorsement. Also, with the computer endorsement, I wrote a letter saying that I had extensive experience in computers from high school through college, including other military and merchant vessels. This letter explained the equivalence of my computer training and I was granted the endorsement.

Always use your resources to get what you need. There are usually legitimate alternatives to actually having to take a class for an endorsement. You might already qualify for some of them. Make sure that equivalency letters detail exactly what the company, vessel, or union wants it to say. Don't make it up. Ask for details: tonnage, time, job responsibilities. Make sure it gets to the right people and follow up to ensure that you have the endorsement in your file. If you do not have equivalent experience or training and have to take the extra classes, it is up to you to complete these classes. Some of the classes are rarely offered and you might have to pay out-of-pocket if you have not worked for that union or company before. Look at it this way, you can go with a company that does not require a lot of extra endorsements and you won't have to worry, or you can bite the bullet, and take the extra classes.

Schools

This last section is about the maritime training schools that offer the classes you need. The USCG has made it easier than ever to find out which schools are approved to teach which classes. On the USCG Web site http://www.uscg.mil/stcw is a section called "merchant mariner info center," which I mentioned earlier. Click on it and a pull-down box will display five or six options. Click on the "approved courses," and a menu will appear listing all courses approved by the USCG. This list is programmed by class. Click on any class or program you need and it will list which schools provide it, contact information, and a description of each class. If you want to shop by schools, go to the USCG home page and click on "New Mariners." Then click on "where to begin," and it will list all of the schools, including all the merchant marine academies, union schools, and private institutes that offer maritime training programs. I recommend that you stick to this list. If you have a question about a particular school, contact the USCG and ask them whether that school is approved for the class. Enough training facilities are available that you can complete your training at one or more of them if needed. The mission statement is to be proactive and ask questions to make sure you are ready with all documentation and training when it is time to go to work. It is all about the certificates these days. If you need them, make sure you have them.

The maritime academies are the other way to get your license. These are four-year college programs that offer a combination of classes, student cruises, and academics, leaving the mariner after four years (or more depending on the student) with a third mate's license and a four-year college degree.

I will now make my official "hawsepiper vs. academy grad" statement: We need each other. The business should be a matrix of both, to bring together working experience and formal education. I have seen good and bad hawsepipers and good and bad academy grads. If you interested in the maritime industry out of high school or a couple years out of high school, and if it is a viable option, meaning you have the grades and the financial backing, go to an academy. This will set you in the workplace with a third mate's license and a four-year degree at a young age. It is worth the investment early in life because it pays off in the long run. I have sailed with academy grads who were captains at the age of twenty-five with unlimited master's licenses.

If you have been in the industry for a number of years, get the sea time you need and get those classes through the hawsepipe. At a point, it becomes inefficient to spend money and time to go back to a four-year academy to get a license you might only need one or two more years to complete. These are merely opinions, of course; you should do whatever you see fit for your own career.

One other exception: If you already have a degree and want to go to an academy just for the license, talk to the academies. They have continuing education programs or master's programs that will allow you to get just the license.

I enlisted in the Coast Guard out of high school. After four years' enlistment, I received my limited tonnage merchant marine deck license with the sea time gained through the Coast Guard. By that time, I only needed seven more months sea time to qualify for my unlimited license as third mate. For me, going to a four-year academy when I only needed seven months sea time would have been inefficient. Weigh all your options before deciding. Your only choice may be to start as an ordinary seaman. It does not matter, as long as you have a plan to upgrade the entire time.

The list of academies and contact information also is included on the Web site (New Mariners—where to begin). The seven major maritime academies, listed in no particular order, are:

- U.S. Merchant Marine Academy—Kings Point, New York
- Maine Maritime Academy—Castine, Maine
- State University of New York Maritime College (SUNY)—Throgs Neck, New York
- Texas Maritime Academy, A&M University at Galveston—Galveston, Texas
- Cal Maritime, California State University—Vallejo, California
- Massachusetts Maritime Academy—Buzzard's Bay, Massachusetts
- Great Lakes Maritime Academy (Northwestern Michigan College)—Traverse City, Michigan

Chapter Five
Navigating the Paperwork: Who Enforces the Law?

One of the enjoyments of being a merchant mariner is the time spent "on the beach." Having completed the required task of your contract or voyage, you are free to enjoy the fruits of your labor by taking extended periods of time off between ships. The last thing mariners want to get saddled with is confusing Coast Guard and STCW requirements while they are spending time off ship.

The Coast Guard is just the messenger of these regulations and is merely responsible for enforcing them, not creating them. This makes for confusion when you want some answers. The IMO, to which the United States belongs, issues the rules. The Coast Guard's responsibility is to enforce them and ensure all mariners comply. That is a challenging job and leaves a lot of room for interpretation. Enforcing regulations you did not create is not the best situation, but that is exactly where the Coast Guard found itself on February 1, 2002, when the new regulations of STCW 95 were put into practice. There were a lot of unanswered questions, and mariners found the process very confusing. Accurately enforcing the rules requires a thorough knowledge and understanding of them. But the rules were new and the REC staff was not sufficiently versed in them. It took some time to work out the kinks. For a while, whenever a mariner asked the Coast Guard a question, the Coast Guard would quickly try to decipher the new rules. Too often, mariners would get indirect answers like, "Go to our Web site," or, "Here is our Web address."

USCG staff would hand mariners a little slip of paper with a Web address on it. The mariner would have to locate a computer somewhere and spend half a day searching for an answer among the oodles of information included on the Web site, which, at the time, was really unorganized. It was the Coast Guard's way of deferring the mariner while they got more control on these new rules, and it worked. Today the Coast Guard may still refer to their Web site for answers, but the site is now more directed and detailed, and so is the Coast Guard.

The criticisms in this book regarding the Coast Guard and other governing bodies reflect a collective frustration shared by mariners attempting to satisfy the new requirements for their MMD and license. The rules and regulations have become quite elaborate in the last few years.

The information in this chapter is intended to help mariners obtain, complete, and present the right documents to the right people.

USCG Regional Exam Center (REC)

The department of the Coast Guard that the merchant mariner deals with is called the REC. It is under the auspices of the sector of the city where the REC is located. For example, Sector San Francisco is the merchant branch of the USCG located in that city. The sector conducts all merchant mariner licensing, including the licensing and inspection of merchant vessels. When a merchant mariner has a question regarding rules and regulations, visiting the local REC is the first step. Merchant mariners are usually familiar with this place and know where the closest one is to them. However, mariners should remember that this is a government agency. There are mountains of forms to complete and the paperwork takes a long time to process. Having the correct documents in the right order before heading to the counter at the REC is a good idea. If you make any mistakes on your application, you delay the paperwork and frustrate the people trying to process it. Your file could go into the great government abyss, never to be seen again. It has happened. The more mistakes on the applications and certificates, the less chance of getting what you want. That said, here are rules to follow when navigating the world of Coast Guard paperwork:

First rule: *Do not mail anything to the Coast Guard unless it is absolutely necessary.* This alleviates any mistakes that could be made in mailing and prevents delay in the application for MMDs and licenses. Physically hand your file to the REC. This ensures that your documents get to where they are going and that you get a visual confirmation of delivery. If that cannot be done due to location, job responsibility or other constraints, talk to someone at your REC, get a name in that office and specifically speak to that person. Tell them what you will be sending them and when. Send the documents registered mail to confirm delivery, and call back to make sure the person at the REC received it. In most cases, RECs deal with original documents only. In the case of mailing original documents, see if certified copies or notarized copies are acceptable. Certified or notarized copies can be made at law offices, banks, and accounting firms, usually for a small fee. The USCG sometimes accepts certified or notarized copies if you mail the documents, but make sure. If you have already established a relationship with a person at the REC, and they have told you to mail paperwork to them, then go ahead and do it per their request. If the REC requests originals only, make sure you get certified or notarized copies of each document for yourself before you mail the originals.

Again, make sure that the recipient's name is on the address as an "attention:" or "attn:" and send it registered mail to ensure proper delivery to the REC. Another big headache that sometimes occurs is that mariners will get an answer from one REC on a question, then go out to sea for a while, return to shore, and stop in at a different REC, only to hear a completely different answer. This anomaly is very real and very frustrating. Therefore, the second rule is: *Stay with one REC.* If you are filing for the first time, for example, in San Francisco (Oakland), then that should be your REC all through your career. Do not transfer your file to another REC unless absolutely necessary. Ask all questions at the REC you know. That way the answers will be consistent and most reliable. If you do find yourself in a different part of the country and cannot contact the REC where your file is located, make sure you create a paper trail with whomever you speak. Write down the names of the people who give you the information.

Do not move your REC file from place to place depending on your job or place of residence. It will cause more headaches in the long run. People move, marry, divorce, travel, and live out of the country, especially merchant mariners. It is not illegal to switch RECs, just make sure your file is sent from an individual at one REC to an individual at the REC of choice. Have a conference call with both RECs to make sure everything is spelled right and sent properly. Also, ask whether the REC will allow you to transfer the file yourself, relieving them of the task of mailing it. In my experience, the USCG does not like to transfer files to another REC, but it does not mean they will not do it or it cannot be done.

You also can submit an application at one REC while your file is at another, as long as you submit everything they need to complete the transaction. The REC usually will contact the other one to make sure your file is in order.

Most mariners know the "people at the front desk." These are the folks at the REC who answer your questions, take documents from you to put in your file, and print your MMDs and licenses. They can be nice, but they also can be a pain. Third rule: *Form a relationship with the Coast Guard.* Now that you have chosen your REC, get to know people there. Remember, a lot of the REC employees are not USCG personnel. It is your responsibility to do the homework. Learn as much as you can about the people at the front desk. Find out who has the experience and can get things done and really understands what you're talking about. Get to know them, introduce yourself, smile, and exchange pleasantries. You have no idea how much this person can help you. Be polite and humble, but persistent. Above all, get their e-mail address. This allows you to bypass the front desk and get the answers you need. Most of the USCG personnel evaluating your applications are online and will send you your approval by e-mail. *Keep their e-mail address.* The addresses are very hard to get, and they give you a pipeline straight to the people who have the answers, or knows who does.

I cannot stress enough the importance of being prepared. Always ask questions, even if you think you are done asking questions, ask more questions. If you feel you are lacking in knowledge of subject matter, talk to a maritime school or visit the Coast Guard Web site prior to walking in and talking to them.

The current contact information of the RECs from the USCG Web site is listed below. Each REC is different. Some are faster at processing your requests than others.

Whichever REC you choose, remember the three rules:
1. Do not mail anything unless absolutely necessary.
2. Stay with one REC
3. Form a relationship with someone at the REC who can get things done for you.

USCG Regional Examination Centers

U.S. Coast Guard
Marine Safety Office
Regional Examination Center
800 E. Dimond Blvd., Suite 3227
Anchorage, AK 99515
Telephone: (907) 271-6736

U.S. Coast Guard
Marine Safety Office
Regional Examination Center
2760 Sherwood, Suite 2A
Juneau, AK 99801-8545
Telephone: (907) 463-2450

U.S. Coast Guard
Marine Safety Office
Regional Examination Center
501 W. Ocean Blvd., Suite 6200
Long Beach, CA 90802
Telephone: (562) 495-1480

U.S. Coast Guard
Regional Examination Center
Oakland Federal Bldg., North Tower
1301 Clay Street, Room 180N
Oakland, CA 94612-5200
Telephone: (510) 637-1124
Fax: (510) 637-1126
E-mail: recsfbay@d11.uscg.mil

U.S. Coast Guard
Regional Examination Center
Claude Pepper Federal Building
51 S.W. 1st Ave., 6th Floor
Miami, FL 33130-1608
Telephone: (305) 536-6548/6874

U.S. Coast Guard
Marine Safety Office
Regional Examination Center
433 Ala Moana Blvd.
Honolulu, HI 96813-4909
Telephone: (808) 522-8264

U.S. Coast Guard
Marine Safety Office
Regional Examination Center
New Orleans
2010 Old Hammond Highway
Metairie, LA 70005
Telephone: (504) 846-6190
Fax: (504) 219-2713

U.S. Coast Guard
Regional Examination Center
U.S. Customs House
40 South Gay Street
Baltimore, MD 21202-4022
Telephone: (410) 962-5132

U.S. Coast Guard
Marine Safety Office
Regional Examination Center
455 Commercial Street
Boston, MA 02109-1045
Telephone: (617) 223-3040

U.S. Coast Guard
Marine Safety Office
Regional Examination Center
1222 Spruce Street, Suite 8.104E
St. Louis, MO 63103-2835
Telephone: (314) 539-3091

U.S. Coast Guard
Activities New York
Regional Examination Center
Battery Park Building
1 South Street
New York, NY 10004-1466
Telephone: (212) 668-7492

U.S. Coast Guard
Regional Examination Center
420 Madison Ave., Suite 700
Toledo, OH 43604
Telephone: (419) 418-6010

USCG Regional Examination Centers (contd.)

U.S. Coast Guard
Marine Safety Office
Regional Examination Center
6767 N. Basin Avenue
Portland, OR 97217-3992
Telephone: (503) 240-9346

U.S. Coast Guard
Marine Safety Office
Regional Examination Center
196 Tradd Street
Charleston, SC 29401-1899
Telephone: (843) 724-7693

U.S. Coast Guard
Marine Safety Office Memphis
Regional Examination Center
200 Jefferson Ave., Suite 1302
Memphis, TN 38103
Telephone: (901) 544-3297

U.S. Coast Guard
Regional Examination Center
8876 Gulf Freeway, Suite 200
Houston, TX 77017-6595
Telephone: (713) 948-3350

U.S. Coast Guard
Marine Safety Office
Regional Examination Center
915 Second Ave., Room 194
Seattle, WA 98174-1067
Telephone: (206) 220-7327

GUAM
U.S. Coast Guard
Regional Examination Center
PSC 455 BOX 176
FPO, GU 96540
Telephone: (671) 355-4900
Fax: (671) 355-4888

Once you have found the REC most convenient for you, every transaction made with the Coast Guard will require some or all of the following items: an application, drug test, physical, two passport photos, fingerprints, a background check, and two forms of identification.

Application

When you are ready to apply to the USCG for any license, document, or endorsement, you will need to fill out an application. The application packet is available on the Coast Guard Web site. Go to the merchant mariner licensing and documentation page (http://www.uscg.mil/STCW/) and click on the "Merchant Mariner info" tab on the left. Scroll down to "application and forms download" and click on it. A list of forms will be displayed, including the application (form CG-719B). If you do not have computer access, you can request an application packet from any REC in person or they can mail it to you. Make sure it is filled out completely and signed before submitting it. Also, make sure you have all the information that the application forms instruct you to bring.

Drug Testing

If you have stepped foot onboard a vessel or done anything in the Department of Transportation (DOT), you probably are familiar with the DOT preemployment and random drug testing. This program ensures that mariners, and the companies they work for, comply with the CFR regarding the transportation industry.

The drug tests are put in place to make sure chronic users of drugs and alcohol are not driving around the highways or navigating waterways as part of their professions. Putting those under the influence of drugs and alcohol on a vessel presents an extreme danger and a huge liability to companies if an accident happens and someone tests positive at the scene. Words of advice: Be a professional in everything you do. If you cannot pass a drug test, then stop reading this book right now and take up another profession.

It is an unfortunate reality that some folks will test positive for drugs or alcohol or both. Many mariners have lost their jobs because of it.

In my opinion, the USCG's general attitude toward mariners is that they really do not want to take your license or documents away. However, when you test positive for drugs or alcohol, you are effectively making them take your papers away. Rehabilitation programs are available for mariners with drug and alcohol problems. The USCG would rather rehabilitate you then send you looking for a new profession. So, not all is lost. They will work with you, but you have to show them that you are worth it. Think of it as a crime—the more severe the incident, the worse the punishment. The USCG Policy Letters (which can be found on the USCG Web site) detail the requirements for the drug screening upon applying to the Coast Guard for your license or MMD.

Get familiar with the term "chain of custody." This means that whoever pays for the drug test, reserves the rights to the results.

If the drug test is part of a pre-employment test, the company will not allow the results to go to any other entity, including you or the USCG. This is why you can obtain approved letters from your company or union stating that you have been part of a random drug testing program and have never tested positive or refused a test.

The details are found in the Coast Guard Web site at http://www.uscg.mil/STCW/ Merchant Mariner Licensing and Documentation. Go to the menu bar on the left-hand side and click on "DRUG TEST INFO." It details the requirements of the drug test, how to prove you are free of dangerous drugs, and the different options for getting that proof. Read the expiration dates on your drug test or drug-free card. You do not want an expired drug test to hold up your application. A drug test or approved letter of random drug testing is good for six months from the date of origination.

The USCG has changed its policy regarding drug-testing letters. The USCG had received fraudulent letters, which had to be from the Medical Review Officers (MROs). A notarized letter will no longer do. It has to come from the lab itself. This is a chain of custody issue that you have to overcome. The company or union that the mariner is taking the test for must send a request to the lab to share the results with the USCG. This request form is mailed with the drug test specimen. When the results are in, the lab's MRO sends the results to a person who has the rights within the chain of custody, i.e., the union, company, or ship. At the same time, the MRO processes the request of a separate results letter that can be used at the USCG. This letter can be mailed to the mariner's home address or the company or union paying for the drug test. The mariner usually has either option. I recommend that you have it mailed to your home address, then hand deliver it and your application to the USCG.

Ensuring that drug-testing letters get to the right people is just another headache to deal with in getting your license or MMD. Ask your union or company officials about the separate MRO letter for the USCG. Talk to the USCG to make sure you have the right information regarding drug tests. They might accept a drug letter from your company or union or they might require a separate one from the MRO. It depends on which REC you apply at. Here is an example taken from the CG Web Site for a Marine Employer:

"APPLICANT'S NAME / SSN passed a chemical test for dangerous drugs, required under Title 46 CFR 16.210 within the previous six months of the date of this letter with no subsequent positive drug test results during the remainder of the six month period."

Here is an example from an Active Military Command or a Government Civilian Command:

"APPLICANT'S NAME / SSN has been subject to a random testing program meeting the criteria of Title 46 CFR 16.230 for at least 60 days during the previous 185 days and has not failed nor refused to participate in a chemical test for dangerous drugs."

Or "APPLICANT'S NAME / SSN has been subject to a random testing program and has never refused to participate in or failed a chemical drug test for dangerous drugs."

If you choose one of the options and have a letter from the company that details your participation in random drug screening and never testing positive, make sure that the letter is written verbatim from the example above. It cannot be different in any way or the USCG might not accept it as valid.

Truth and accuracy regarding drug-testing letters is very important to the mariner, and it is our responsibility to make sure that the company or union official knows this and writes the letter correctly. When in doubt, write the letter yourself, and save it to a disk or CD, then let the company official proof it against the CFR and USCG regulations, print it on company letterhead, and sign it. The latest and greatest regarding drug testing is the induction of the MRO, or medical review officer.

A few years ago, some mariners took it upon themselves to forge their own drug-free letters and the USCG caught them. The few who could not play by the rules have made it more difficult for everyone else.

The way to find the MRO's contact info is to look in the upper-right-hand side of the drug testing form. The MRO's name, office address and phone number should be on it. Write that down. You might be able to talk to the MRO personally and tell them what you need. If all else fails, you can always pay for a separate drug test yourself and bring it to the USCG. A drug test is good for six months from the date of the results.

Physicals

USCG medical physical examinations are easy to understand, for now. A medical physical is good for one year from the date of the physical, not from the date you turn it in to the USCG with your application.

The USCG physical examination form is in the application packet, which you can download from the USCG Web site for free. It is available on the USCG Web site http://www.uscg.mil/STCW/. Click on the "applications and forms" link. You will see a list of forms to download, including form CG-719K "Merchant Mariner Physical Examination Report." This form can be taken to any licensed physician, physician's assistant, or nurse practitioner.

In my experience, most private doctors' offices are not familiar with this form. You have to explain what it is and what it is used for, and then they usually comply with the unusual paperwork. Occupational medical centers are more familiar with the USCG physicals. If you are with a company or union that requires you to have a physical before you are employed (i.e., unions, military, tanker companies) you cannot use these medical examinations as USCG physicals. Believe me, I've tried. It is a chain of custody issue again. I belonged to the SIU while I was sailing as an AB and taking some upgrading classes at their facility in Maryland.

The SIU, like other unions, requires an annual physical to qualify for benefits and to sail with them. If you sail a certain amount of time with them, they will pay for your drug test and physical. I, thinking ahead, brought my USCG form with me to the physical hoping the doctor could fill it out while she was filling out my union physical. As I handed her the forms, she said she would be happy to fill them out, as long as I paid for it separately. I played dumb and said I thought she could fill these USCG forms out too. She said she could, but needed to get paid for it; after all, she was a doctor doing two separate tasks. This disappointed me, but I understood where she was coming from. I knew the USCG would not accept my union physical. Upon the doctor's instruction, I went back to my union to pay for the additional physical paperwork. The union representative looked at me and said, "Why didn't you just tell me you needed a Coast Guard physical as well?"

"I didn't know I had to," I responded.

He printed out the request, which, because of my time spent in the union, was paid for by the union, and I took it back to the doctor, and within the hour I had both physicals and did not have to pay a dime. On the next page is an example of the USCG physical examination form. Included with it are instructions for filling it out. These forms are easily printed out from the USCG Web site for free. If you do not have access to a computer or are not the Silver Surfer of the Internet, go into your local REC and ask for a physical examination form (CG-719K). They have every document you need, but a computer can save you a trip to the REC. Again, make sure you know what you are talking about before you go in. You do not want to play the runaround game.

If you are applying for a raise in grade on your license or MMD, meaning you are getting a bigger, better license, the physical you submitted for the original license is good for three years upon application for your raise-in-grade. So if you upgrade your license within those three years you do not have to get another physical. One less thing to do.

Also, the newest requirements to date coming down from the National Maritime Center are the full explanation of the medical requirements for mariners obtaining licenses and MMDs. The chief mate on my last ship, Mike Lee, made me aware of this. It is a National Vessel Inspection Circular (NVIC), which the NMC writes periodically with new updates to regulations. The NVIC is still in draft form, but I have read it. It does not have a designation yet, but is titled, "Medical and Physical Evaluation Guidelines for Merchant Mariner Credentials."

This is a guideline for the medical industry to evaluate each mariner by ensuring that proper medical evaluation is given. It is a pretty in-depth document, which explains what mariners need medical waivers for. The physical requirements have not changed, and the USCG physical form CG-719K and E (for entry level ratings) are still valid. This document merely serves as a reference for medical personnel to ensure the physical is conducted properly.

That does not mean the USCG physical form (719K /E) will not change later. Regulations and requirements are getting tougher, and medical requirements are no different. The military is doing it as well, so the USCG is following suite with the merchant marines. Be aware of these changes and be prepared for medical requirements to become harder.

Department of Transportation U.S. Coast Guard CG-719K (Rev 1/02)	**Merchant Mariner Physical Examination Report**	OMB-2115-0514 **Page 1**

Instructions

If you are applying for:

1. **ORIGINAL LICENSE AND/OR QUALIFIED RATING DOCUMENT** (i.e., *First Rating* of Able Seaman, Qualified Member of the Engine Department, and Tankerman) – Submit this report, completed by your physician.

2. **RENEWAL OF LICENSE AND/OR QUALIFIED RATING DOCUMENT** – You may:
   - **Submit this report, completed by your physician; or**
   - **Submit a certification by a physician in accordance with Title 46, CFR, 10.209(d) or 12.02-27(d).**

3. **RAISE-IN-GRADE (LICENSES)** – You may:
   - **Submit this report, completed by your physician; or**
   - **Submit a certification by a physician in accordance with Title 46, CFR, 10.207(e).**

Instructions for Licensed Physician / Physician Assistant / Nurse Practitioner

The U. S. Coast Guard requires a physical examination / certification be completed to ensure that all holders of Licenses and Merchant Mariner Documents are physically fit and free of debilitating illness and injury. Physicians completing the examination should ensure that mariners:

- Are of sound health.
- Have no physical limitations that would hinder or prevent performance of duties.
- Are physically and mentally able to stay alert for 4 to 6-hour shifts.
- Are free from any medical conditions that pose a risk of sudden incapacitation, which would affect operating, or working on vessels.

Below is a partial list of physical demands for performing the duties of a merchant mariner in most segments of the maritime industry:

- Working in cramped spaces on rolling vessels.
- Maintaining balance on a moving deck.
- Rapidly donning an exposure suit.
- Stepping over doorsills of 24 inches in height.
- Opening and closing watertight doors that may weigh up to 56 pounds.
- Pulling heavy objects, up to 50 lbs. in weight, distances of up to 400 feet.
- Climbing steep stairs or vertical ladders without assistance.
- Participating in firefighting and lifesaving efforts, including wearing a self-contained breathing apparatus (SCBA), and lifting/controlling fully charged fire hoses.

1. Detailed guidelines on potentially disqualifying medical conditions are contained in Navigation and Vessel Inspection Circular (NVIC) 02-98. Physicians should be familiar with the guidelines contained within this document. NVIC 02-98 may be obtained from www.uscg.mil/hq/g-m/index or by calling the nearest USCG Regional Examination Center.

2. Examples of physical impairment or medical conditions that could lead to disqualification include impaired vision, color vision or hearing; poorly controlled diabetes; multiple or recent myocardial infarctions; psychiatric disorders; and convulsive disorders. In short, any condition that poses an inordinate risk of sudden incapacitation or debilitating complication, and any condition requiring medication that impairs judgment or reaction time are potentially disqualifying and will require a detailed evaluation.

3. Engineer Officer, Radio Officer, Offshore Installation Manager, Barge Supervisor, Ballast Control Operator, QMED and Tankerman applicants need only to have the ability to distinguish the colors **red**, **green**, **blue** and **yellow**. The physician should indicate in Section IV the method used to determine the applicant's ability to distinguish these colors.

4. This applicant should present photo identification before the physical examination/certification.

Privacy Act Statement

As required by Title 5 United States Code (U.S.C.) 552a(e)(3), the following information is provided when supplying personal information to the U. S. Coast Guard.

1. Authority for solicitation of the information: 46 U.S.C. 2104(a), 7101(c)-(e), 7306(a)(4), 7313(c)(3), 7317(a), 8703(b), 9102(a)(5).

2. Principal purposes for which information is used:
   a. To determine if an applicant is physically capable of performing shipboard duties.
   b. To ensure that a duly licensed Physician/Physician Assistant/Nurse Practitioner conducts the applicant's physical examination/certification and to verify the information as needed.

3. The routine uses which may be made of this information:
   a. This form becomes a part of the applicant's file as documentary evidence that regulatory physical requirements have been satisfied and the applicant is physically competent to hold a merchant mariner license or document.
   b. The information becomes part of the total license or document file and is subject to review by federal agency casualty investigators.
   c. This information may be used by the U. S. Coast Guard and an Administrative Law Judge in determining causation of marine casualties and appropriate suspension and revocation action.

4. Disclosure of this information is voluntary, but failure to provide this information will result in non-issuance of a license and/or merchant mariner's document.

"An agency may not conduct or sponsor, and a person is not required to respond to a collection of information unless it displays a valid OMB control number". The Coast Guard estimates that the average burden for completing this form is 10 minutes. You may submit any comments concerning the accuracy of this burden estimate or any suggestion for reducing the burden to the; Commandant (G-CIM), U.S. Coast Guard, 2100 2nd Street, SW, Washington, DC 20593-0001 or Office of Management and Budget, Paperwork Reduction Project (2115-0514), Washington, DC 20503.

Section I – Applicant Information

Name (Last, First, Middle) of Applicant

Date of Birth (Month, Day, Year)   Social Security Number

Section II - Physical Information

| Eye Color | Hair Color | Weight ___ lbs | Distinguishing Marks |

| Height ___ ft ___ in | Blood Pressure Systolic ___ / Diastolic ___ | Pulse Resting ___ ☐ Regular ☐ Irregular |

Section III - Vision (if you have corrected vision, BOTH uncorrected & corrected MUST be shown)

UNCORRECTED	CORRECTABLE TO	FIELD OF VISION
Right 20 / ___	Right 20 / ___	☐ Normal
Left 20 / ___	Left 20 / ___	☐ Abnormal

The applicant must have **100** degrees horizontal field of vision

Section IV – Color Vision

☐ PASS   ☐ FAIL   Deck Officers/Ratings (masters, mates, pilots, operators, able-seaman) must be tested using one of the following tests. For all other licenses/ratings, see page 1, note 3.

Pseudoisochromatic Plates

☐ Divorine - 2nd Edition

☐ AOC

☐ AOC Revised Edition

☐ AOC - HRR

☐ Ishihara 16, 24, 38 Plate Edition

☐ Eldridge - Green Perception Lantern

☐ Farnsworth Lantern (FALANT)

☐ Keystone Orthoscope

☐ Keystone Telebinocular

☐ SAMCTT- School of Aviation Medicine

☐ Titmus Optical Vision Test

☐ Williams Lantern

Section V - Hearing

☐ NORMAL   ☐ IMPAIRED (If impaired, complete Audiometer and Functional Speech Discrimination Test)

Audiometer (Threshold Value)	500 Hz	1000 Hz	2000 Hz	3000 Hz
Right Ear (Unaided)				
Left Ear (Unaided)				
Right Ear (Aided)				
Left Ear (Aided)				

Functional Speech Discrimination Test at 55 dB	Right Ear (Unaided) ___ %	Left Ear (Unaided) ___ %
	Right Ear (Aided) ___ %	Left Ear (Aided) ___ %

Section VI - Medications

List all current medications, including dosage and possible side effects. State the condition(s) for which the medication(s) are taken.

☐ NO PRESCRIPTION MEDICATIONS

Department of Transportation U.S. Coast Guard CG-719K (Rev 1/02)	**Merchant Mariner Physical Examination Report**	OMB-2115-0514 **Page 4**

Section VII – Certification of Physical Impairment or Medical Conditions

Does the applicant have or ever suffered from any of the following? **IF YES, PROVIDE TEST RESULTS, AS INDICATED.**	**If YES:**	• Identify the condition • Any limitations • Is condition controlled	• Date of diagnosis • Prognosis

Yes	No		Remarks (Please Print)
		1. Circulatory System	
		a. Heart disease (**Stress Test within the past year**)	
		b. Hypertension (**Recent BP reading**)	
		c. Chronic renal failure	
		d. Cardiac surgery (**Stress Test within the past year**)	
		e. Blood disorder/vascular disease	
		2. Digestive System	
		a. Severe digestive disorder	
		3. Endocrine System	
		a. Thyroid dysfunction (**TSH level within the past year**)	
		b. Diabetes (**State effects on vision & HgbAlc w/in 30 days**)	
		4. Infectious	
		a. Communicable disease	
		b. Hepatitis A, B or C	
		c. HIV	
		d. Tuberculosis	
		5. Mental System	
		a. Psychiatric disorder	
		b. Depression	
		c. Attempted suicide	
		d. Alcohol abuse	
		e. Drug abuse	
		f. Loss of memory	
		6. Musculoskeletal System	
		a. Amputations	
		b. Impaired range of motion	
		c. Impaired balance/coordination	
		7. Nervous System	
		a. Epilepsy/seizure	
		b. Dizziness/unconsciousness	
		c. Paralysis	
		8. Respiratory System	
		a. Asthma (**PFT results within the past year**)	
		b. Lung disease (**PFT results within the past year**)	
		9. Other	
		a. Debilitating allergies	
		b. Other eye disease (**Corrected/Uncorrected Visual acuity**)	
		c. Glaucoma (**Pressure test results within the past year**)	
		d. Recent or repetitive surgery	
		e. Sleepwalking	
		f. Severe speech impediment	
		g. Other illness or disability not listed	

Considering the findings in this examination, and noting the physical demands that may be placed upon the applicant, I consider the applicant **(please check one)**	☐ Competent	☐ Not competent	☐ Needing further review

Name of Physician/Physician Assistant/Nurse Practitioner	License Number	Telephone Number	Office Address, City, State, Zip
Signature of Physician/Physician Assistant/Nurse Practitioner	**Date**		

I certify that all information provided by me is complete and true to the best of my knowledge

X **Signature of Applicant**   Date

Passport Photos and Passports

For most USCG transactions, two passport photos are required. Supplying the photos is your responsibility. Make sure you know whether you will need these photos. If your transaction warrants passport photos, do not go into the Coast Guard without them. I always have passport photos with me, as should you.

Sometimes the USCG can take the photos for you at the REC, but do not rely on this. Ask them beforehand if that service is available. A United States passport also is important to shipping. Most companies require U.S. passports to get a job on an oceangoing vessel. Renewing your passport can be a pain, but you can download forms from the Internet and do it by mail, if you qualify.

Here is an excerpt from a *Master Mates and Pilots Weekly Newsletter* written by a member with some good information on passport renewals:

PASSPORT RENEWAL AVAILABLE AT NO CHARGE

MM&P member Ken Welch advises that members about to renew their U.S. passport can save some money by getting their renewal at no charge. Welch recently renewed his passport using this method free of charge. The only problem he encountered was originally enclosing a letter from the union instead of his employer attesting to the fact he was employed on a U.S. registered ship. Once he provided the proper letter, his passport was renewed and returned by overnight Fed-Ex.

Welch writes, "I had contacted several passport issuing agencies around the country but none of them knew anything about the below listed Code of Federal Regulations and/or U.S. Codes. After a lot of searching, I located the only agency that handles these types of issuances or renewals. It is the same agency that issues diplomatic passports. As it turned out, my employer handles this matter for their overseas employees on a fairly routine basis and was quite familiar with the procedure."

You will need to provide:
1. Current valid passport

---

2. Two passport quality photos
3. An ORIGINAL signed letter on your employer's company letterhead confirming your employment on a U.S. registered ship.
4. Photocopy (front and back) of your USCG merchant marine license.
5. Photocopy (front and back) of your USCG MMD (Z-card).
6. Application for passport renewal, Form DS-82.

Unlicensed personnel should contact the issuing agency to determine other required documentation. Anyone can call and verify all this information beforehand should you have any questions. Allow 4-6 weeks for processing, but, if you have not received your new passport after about 3 weeks, you should call their office to inquire. Bearing in mind the poor USPS service, I strongly suggest you certify your packet of documents, or send them via UPS or Fed-Ex.

The address to send the information to is:

Passport Office - Special Issuance Agency
Attn: Special Assistance Department
1111 19TH Street NW, Room 200
Washington, DC 20036
Tel: (202) 955-0198
Fax: (202) 955-0182

1. You can pick up a passport renewal form (DS-82) at any US post-office or passport office. Or, download one from numerous sites such as: http://travel.state.gov/passport/forms/ds82/ds82_843.html where you can even complete it online before printing.
2. 22CFR22.1.4b can be found at: http://www.gpoaccess.gov/cfr/retrieve.html
3. 22USC214 can be found at: http://techlawreporter.com/toa/codes/usc/titles/TITLE22/22USC214.html
Other US Code of Federal Regulations sections pertaining to No-Fee Passports include:
22CFR13.1 - Improper exaction of fees
22CFR22.6 - Refund of fees
For more info, email Welch at kgscwelch@juno.com .

Be aware that a no-fee passport is not a tourist passport. It is valid for work on U.S. merchant ships only. It is good only for five years, instead of the standard ten years for a tourist passport. The no-fee passport has a stamp on the back saying it is for work only, not tourist travel.

I followed the procedures and received a no-fee passport. The only problem I encountered was the issuing agency mistook my application for a no-fee diplomatic passport, which is red and reserved for diplomats. I spoke to the agent and clarified that I needed a blue no-fee passport. It was resolved and I received my new passport promptly. I recommend putting the word "blue" on your application DS-82 when you send it in to Washington D.C. to avoid the confusion.

Fingerprints

If you have not already been, you will be fingerprinted at the REC when you go in to submit your paperwork. This is done with most original licenses and documents. It does not mean that you will not be fingerprinted if you go in for something else, like a renewal or upgrade, but if the USCG has your fingerprints already, they usually will not fingerprint you again. Security has increased in the shipping industry, which is why the USCG now operates under the Department of Homeland Security. If you have not been fingerprinted in a while, the USCG might do it again. They have everything at the REC, even those handy-wipes to clean your hands after you are done. Fingerprinting is strictly the USCG's call. Do what they say to do.

I believe that you can now get your fingerprints done at other places, like the UPS Store. Before you do, speak to the USCG to make sure they will accept fingerprints that were done off site.

Background Checks

A background check is conducted for any original license or document, upgrade or renewal. It usually takes one to three weeks, depending on how backed-up the paperwork is at your REC. Make sure to ask how long the background checks are taking. This will give you a timeline for when things will get done. When you apply to the USCG, your background check will begin its process. If all goes well, the evaluation of your application and the background check will be done at the same time. Try not to let your background check hold up your application.

A very important thing: Do not lie on your application for any reason. The background checks now involve the Federal Bureau of Investigation (FBI) and the Department of Motor Vehicles (DMV). The USCG will know more about you than you do when they are done. If they find that you have lied on your application, they will deny you any merchant mariner's documents, period. No one likes to admit they made a mistake. This is really only a problem when it comes to felonies, convictions, and any illegal activity. The USCG wants to know it all, so do not leave anything out on the application. Believe me, I have sailed with mariners who had hefty rap sheets. They were upfront with the USCG and attached all the pertinent paperwork with the application for their license and MMD. After these were checked, the USCG approved them for their documents because they had come clean and had documented everything. The way to look at this aspect of the application process is if it does not look right or is not in order, the USCG probably won't go for it. Do not withhold information, and make sure everything is legitimate. The USCG follows 46CFR 10.201, which is eligibility for all licenses and certificates. Consult the CFR Web Site and read this passage to ensure accuracy regarding criminal convictions.

I heard a story about a mariner applying for his MMD, and he said he did not have any felonies. The USCG cross-referenced his background check with the FBI and found that he had a Driving While Intoxicated (DWI). They denied his application, not because of the DWI, but because he lied on his application. Any USCG document is an official government document and it is illegal to lie on them. I cannot stress enough, do not lie on any of your documents. If you have any doubts or questions, make sure to ask. A background check, once completed, is good for at least one year. That means if you have any business with the USCG within that year, you can let them know you have an existing background check, and they only need to e-mail a request to reopen it. It should take only one to three days.

Forms of Identification/Citizenship

You need to bring identification for the USCG: Two pieces to prove you are who you say you are, and one for proof of citizenship or resident alien status. Some of the pieces of ID can double as two proofs. For example, a U.S. passport doubles as identification (photo and information) and citizenship (U.S. government document).

Again, these pieces of ID are original licenses and documents, but don't be without them. Do not bring copies of these documents. The USCG might not accept copies unless you are mailing them. I have a briefcase with me at all times that contains everything applicable in this chapter, all originals (including four pieces of ID). Things go so much more smoothly when you are over-prepared.

For acceptable forms of ID, go to the USCG Web site and click on "Checklist" in the toolbar on the left. Scroll down to "Acceptable forms of ID" and click on it. A list will appear that details all the ID requirements, what you can and cannot use for ID. At least one of the documents provided must be from the "photo ID" section.

If your application has to be mailed, it may be mailed with the above documents. However, if you must go to the REC to be fingerprinted, you can present the original proof of identification instead of mailing it. For new MMDs, mariners are required to show their original Social Security Card prior to issuance. This takes care of the proof of citizenship. Most new mariners come in with their birth certificate, social security card and driver's license.

User Fees for all Licenses and Documents

This section lists all the fees that apply for anything dealing with the USCG. There usually is an evaluation fee, a testing fee, and an issuance fee. Make sure you have the ability to pay these exactly, be it by check, cash, or credit. Like any business, the USCG will deny anything unpaid.

I'll end this chapter with a list from the USCG Web site of the top ten reasons licensing is delayed. Do not let any of these happen to you.

Applications—If the application is not completed, it will be returned for correction. Three signatures are mandatory: Section III ("Have you ever...?" questions), Section V (consent of

Table 5.1. Fees

If you apply for	Evaluation fee	And you need Examination then the fee is	Issuance then the fee is
Original License			
Upper level	$100	$110	$45
Lower level	$100	$95	$45
Raise of grade	$100	$45	$45
Modification or removal of limitation or scope			
Endorsement	$50	$45	$45
Renewal	$50	$45	$45
Renewal for continuity Purposes	n/a	n/a	$45
Reissue, Replacement, and Duplicate	n/a	n/a	$145
Radio Officer License			
Original	$50	n/a	$45
Endorsement	$50	$45	$45
Renewal	$50	n/a	$45
Renewal for continuity Purposes	n/a	n/a	$45
Reissue, Replacement, and Duplicate	n/a	n/a	$145
Certificate of Registry			
Original (MMD holder)	$90	n/a	$45
Original (MMD applicant)	$105	n/a	$45
Renewal	$50	n/a	$45
Renewal for continuity Purposes	n/a	n/a	$45
Endorsement	n/a	n/a	$45
Reissue, Replacement, and Duplicate	n/a	n/a	$145

Table continued

Table 5.1. cont'd. Fees

If you apply for	Evaluation fee	And you need Examination then the fee is	Issuance then the fee is
STCW Certification			
Original	No fee	No fee	No fee
Renewal	No fee	No fee	No fee

1 Duplicate for document lost as result of marine casualty. No Fee.

National Driver Registry check), and Section VI (application certification). When the "Applying for:" block is left blank or is incomplete, the REC is left to guess what you want.

Drug Screen—A drug screen is often rejected because it does not contain the Medical Review Officer's (MRO) signature, it is a photocopy, or a company compliance letter is not written to meet the requirements of the Code of Federal Regulations, Title 46, Part 16, Section 220.

Photographs—Merchant Mariner's Documents (MMDs) and STCW certificates cannot be printed without a photograph. Two passport-size photos are needed when applying for an MMD or STCW.

Physical Exam—If the Merchant Marine Personnel Physical Examination/Certification Report is not complete, it will be returned for correction. Particular attention is paid to the "competent," "not competent," and "needs further review" boxes, which frequently are left blank. Often the type of color vision exam given in Section IV in not indicated or mariners who wear glasses and/or contacts submit exams without their uncorrected vision listed in Section III.

Original Certificates—Photocopies of essential documents, even if notarized, are not accepted. Only original signatures, those documents signed by the issuing authority (e.g., course completion certificates) or official custodian (e.g., birth certificates) are acceptable. Original certificates will be returned when the evaluation is completed and the REC mails the newly issued credentials to the applicant.

User Fees—No or incorrect fees are included with the application. Licensing user fees changed as of October 4, 1999. Current fees are published in the most recent Code of Federal Regulations, Title 46, Part 10, Section 109 and on the web at: http://www.uscg.mil/STCW/l-userfees.htm.

Current or Past License, Document, and/or STCW—A mariner who is holding, or has held, a license, MMD, and/or STCW certificate who does not indicate it in the history (Section II of the application) or does not include a copy of their credentials (front and back) with the application package. This especially applies for renewals and mariners with past transactions at other RECs.

Sea Service—Missing or conflicting information on the sea service letter (e.g., not including tonnage or horsepower, the position listed does not agree with other documents in the application package, or conflicting waters). Service should be documented with discharges, letters from marine employers, or small boat sea service forms. If a small boat service form is used, it must be certified and signed by the owner or proof of individual ownership is required.

Written Statement—If an applicant marks "Yes" in any block of Section III, a written statement is required. Note that all questions beginning with "Have you ever..." include all past convictions, even ones that may have already been disclosed. Simply stating "on file" will not suffice. Statements should include the what, when, where, and penalties assessed for each incident, if it has already been disclosed to the REC, and whether there have been any new incidents. The applicant must sign and date the statement.

Medical Condition—Additional medical information is required whenever a medical condition is identified on the Merchant Marine Personnel Physical Examination Report.

Chapter Six
Practical Assessments

Along with the classes you are required to take, you must complete practical assessments before applying to the REC for a license or MMD.

Explanation of Assessments

This system of practical assessments is derived from the military system called Personal Qualification Standards (PQS). Each job in the military you perform has a list of PQS tasks that must be learned, performed, and signed by a qualified individual before the job can be done. After completing the PQS for a specific job, the individual's commanding officer usually gives an oral board or written test. After completing the PQS and testing, the individual is qualified to do the job and is put to work in that arena. The Coast Guard now has instituted this system for the merchant marines. All the mariner is doing is their PQS to get qualified to do the job. Just like PQS, each assessment has a range of standards to follow, so there is no confusion as to what and how the mariner completes each assessment.

Control Sheet

Each assessment has a sheet explaining everything. That is called its assessment control sheet. Each assessment control sheet has a specific number and letter code. For example, OICNW-1-1A would be the number for the first assessment in the third/second mate's Officer in Charge of a Navigational Watch. The next would be OICNW-1-1B, and so on. Every policy letter that has the assessments in them also comes with an outline of all the assessment control sheets and their codes. This spreadsheet is designed so that you can quickly reference all the control sheets as they are sorted by their control code. Also, the spreadsheet is a helpful tool to ensure that you have all the control sheets you need printed.

Make sure that when you are done printing the policy letter and assessments that pertain to you, you cross reference the outline of assessments with all the assessment control sheets that were printed with it to ensure you have them all. You do not want to board a ship for four months only to discover that you are missing a control sheet for one assessment because it never printed.

Before the installation of STCW 95, a hawsepiper could get a third mate's license without ever practically demonstrating the scope of responsibility that a third mate has onboard a ship. The requirements of a mate's license before STCW 95 was based on a certain amount of sea time and some basic required classes like radar, ARPA, GMDSS, and Basic and Advanced Firefighting. The hawsepiper would have to take a prep class or self-study the remaining subjects to pass the USCG exam.

This lack of practical assessments often led to mates feeling overwhelmed on their first job. They took the reins, only to discover that the true magnitude of their responsibility was much greater than indicated by a couple of classes and passing an exam. I know, because I received my first 1,600-ton mate's license without having to complete practical assessments, and that was how I felt when I found myself responsible for the ship, cargo, and crew on my first watch. I lacked preparation, to say the least. Realistically, the classes plus the sea time only account for a fraction of the knowledge and experience needed to perform the task of a mate in charge of a navigational watch onboard a vessel. As surprising as it may sound, this was the norm for hawsepipers for years until STCW 95 was adopted. STCW 95 requires the hawsepiping mariner to complete certain sets of job-related duties to the satisfaction of a senior officer or qualified classroom assessor.

This scheme is designed to improve the learning curve. The downside is that it is much more difficult to get a merchant mariner's license now with the STCW 95 qualifications. Let's be honest, the overwhelming feeling will always be there the first time you are in charge of the bridge as a new mate.

Even as the scope of responsibility in the maritime industry increases and personnel aboard a vessel decreases, mariners obviously still have a lot to learn; but now they have a better, practice-centered educational base to which to apply it.

For example, an AB might be part of the navigational watch onboard a vessel as a helmsman and a lookout. Being a helmsman requires knowledge of the steering system and helm commands as well as a good "seaman's eye" (the ability to judge steering, navigation and lookout duties of a vessel by experience alone). Also, being the lookout requires basic knowledge of bearings, ranges, lights, shapes, sound signals, radar, and basic ARPA features. This AB is part of the navigational team, but the AB is not ready to take responsibility of a vessel as a third mate relying solely on his experience as an AB.

The practical assessments guide the AB in the fundamentals of the job as a watchstanding mate. These assessments, along with the completion of the required classes, prepare the mariner better than before to stand a proper navigational watch and take responsibility for the vessel. The combination of classes and assessments cover the theory behind the job and the practical execution of that theory.

For example, hawsepipers must take the class Coastal and Terrestrial Navigation. This class teaches the theory behind taking fixes by terrestrial bearings, radar ranges, distance off, bow/beam bearings, and other subjects discussed in chapter four. After completing the class, the mariner has to practically demonstrate competency by taking a fix using visual bearings and radar ranges to the satisfaction of the person evaluating the student (this can be done in an approved classroom setting or onboard a vessel underway with appropriate equipment). Through this process, mariners execute what they have learned to the satisfaction of the assessors and may become assessors themselves, teaching other mariners. The process is supposed to improve the level of knowledge and proficiency on the bridge by all mariners, including the assessors. One of the best ways for an officer to refresh subject matter is by teaching it. All seventy-eight practical assessments for the third/ second mate follow the subject matter outlined in the twenty or so separate classes. It encompasses the fundamentals of bridge watchstanding.

A mariner has three different assessment packages starting at ordinary seaman up to master.
1. The assessments from OS to AB are called "Ratings Forming Part of a Navigational Watch (RFPNW)."
2. The practical assessments from AB to mate are called "Officer in Charge of a Navigational Watch."
3. The assessment package from second mate to chief mate/mas-

ter is titled, "Masters and Chief Mates on Ships of 3,000 Gross Tonnage or More (ITC)."
4. The assessment package specifically for towing vessels is called "The Towing Officer Assessment Record (TOAR)."

Each of these assessment packages will be completed and turned into the Coast Guard with your license or MMD application. These assessments, along with the classes, must be completed and signed before applying for your MMD or license.

The OS to AB RFPNW assessments can be signed in a classroom setting or onboard a ship that has approved equipment. With the practical assessments from OS to AB, make sure that the OS has some understanding and experience for the task of a helmsman and lookout.

On the bridge during normal underway operation, the OS rarely gets to be the helmsman. That job is taken by the AB, who is a qualified helmsman. Previously, when that same OS had enough sea time on deck, he could go to the USCG, take the AB and lifeboat tests, and get an AB ticket. That MMD or Z card qualified the new AB as a helmsman and lookout, having never done the job before. The RFPNW class and assessments make sure that the OS now has some training before becoming an AB.

The AB to mate assessments are, in my opinion, the most difficult to get signed. The AB to mate has the largest number of assessments, and since officers must sign off on many of these, this can be challenging.

Officer in Charge of a Navigational Watch for third/second mate assessments has the highest learning curve of them all, and the subjects are broad-ranging: celestial, terrestrial, electronic and coastal navigation, radar, ARPA, ship handling, emergency procedures, rules of the road, search and rescue, and the list goes on. After completion, the assessments are turned into the USCG, with all the other requirements for a license or MMD application detailed in this book.

Think about this: Would you want a doctor operating on you who had been trained through lecture and textbooks, but had never received any practical experience? Introduce STCW 95 into the scheme. Now the mariner has to do the job, before they get the job, just as other professions require.

The chief mate/master assessment package is easier because there are less of them than the third/second mate (53 vs. 78), and the mariner is now a second mate already and is more familiar with the assessments and bridge responsibilities.

Where to Get the Assessments

All of the practical assessments are inside Coast Guard policy letters as "enclosures." I have mentioned these policy letters before for one reason or another. They are on the Coast Guard Web site and can be viewed, printed, or downloaded for free.

OS to AB assessments are "Ratings Forming Part of a Navigational Watch." Go to the USCG Web page at: www.uscg.mil/stcw/.

On the left-hand side of the site is a menu bar. Click on "Merchant Mariner Info Center" and a new menu bar will appear, click on "Policy and Guidance." Scroll down and click on [14-02]. This is the policy letter that explains the Ratings Forming Part of a Navigational Watch regulations and prerequisites. It also contains the assessments themselves, which can be printed, saved, or downloaded for free. Bind them together and take them onto the next ship, to be worked on and signed by a second mate unlimited or higher. The signing continues throughout this chapter. Make sure the computer you are using has Adobe, because all the USCG policy letters are in PDF format. This program usually is on the computer, but if not, it can be downloaded for free.

Following the same steps from the previous paragraphs regarding the USCG Web site and "Policy and Guidance," click on policy letter: [01-02] the package for 500 ton master up to third/second mate unlimited, the official title of the document is: "NMC Policy Letter No. 01-02. Subject: Applicants for ocean or near coastal mate license for service on vessels of 500 or more gross tonnage (GT) (200 gross registered tons [GRT]) with qualifying service or training beginning on or after 1 August 1998 and all applicants beginning 1 February 2002."

These policy numbers (i.e., [01-02]) represent the sequence in which the policy letters were issued, so this letter is the first (01) of the year 2002 (02). Every policy letter corresponds to a sequence and year. After you click on [01-02], it should consist of forty-five pages and end with an assessment control sheet number OICNW-1-7B. You can save it to a disk or CD, or print it on the spot. After that, go back to the Web site where you clicked on [01-02], and right below it will be [Part 2]. Click on that, and the second part of the assessment sheets will open. The assessment control sheets will continue, beginning with OICNW-1-7C and ending with OICNW-2-3H. Save or print that section, and then click on [Part 3] and do the same thing.

Important: One assessment control sheet could be missing. After you are done with policy letter [01-02]-[Part 2] and [Part 3], scroll down to policy letter [16-02] labeled "Change 1 to NMC Policy Letter [01-02]." Click on [16-02]. In that letter you will find an additional assessment labeled OICNW-2-3C. Save or print this too. Your assessment package will not be complete without it.

The policy letter outlines every requirement you need to fulfill for the license: application, sea time, classes, physicals, drug tests, and assessments. The policy letter attachments, or "enclosures," as the USCG refers to them, are all the assessment control sheets. In total, it is a hefty bundle of paper, but it is crucially important. Carry it wherever you go. I recommend three-hole punching the entire thing, putting it in a hard binder, and labeling it with your name and title. For example: "Leonard Lambert third/second Mate Assessments," or something like that. This binder is a great reference tool, and you never know when somebody will want to sign off your assessments, so keep it with you.

The Chief Mate/Master policy letter is entitled "Masters and Chief Mates on Ships of 3,000 Gross Tonnage or More (ITC)." Follow the same sequence, and click on [04-02]. This is only a one-part letter, so once you have [04-02], you have everything you need. There will be 53 assessments total, from M-1-1A to M-9-1D.

Towing Officer Assessment Record (TOAR)

Towing Officer Assessment Record (TOAR) is a list of assessments designed specifically for towing officers. They are conducted the same way as the other assessments, but are directed toward towing vessels. They can be found in policy letter [04-03] and printed for free from the USCG Web site. TOAR assessments are specific to towing vessels and have their own requirements. Make sure and read the policy letter to understand what is needed to get the towing endorsement on your license.

Getting the Assessments Signed

There are two ways to get the assessments signed. One is by completing the assessments onboard a vessel that has all the required equipment and qualified assessors to teach each assessment to the mariner and sign it. The other is to have the assessments signed in a classroom or "navigational laboratory," as the USCG likes to put it. You can get certain assessments signed that correspond to each class required of the mariner. If the mariner chooses to go the classroom route, by the time they have completed all the classes, all the assessments should be completed and signed from each class. For example, the class Celestial Navigation is anywhere from two to four weeks long, depending on which school you attend. As I talked about before, the mariner will study celestial bodies and how they relate to fixing a ship's position on the earth. In the Officer in Charge of a Navigational Watch practical assessments, five or six pertain to celestial navigation. If the school teaching the Celestial Navigation class has been approved by the USCG and NMC to issue the STCW Celestial Navigation certificate and to sign the celestial navigation assessments in the class, then part of that class should entail the students completing the practical assessments. The Celestial Navigation class I took at the SIU maritime school in Piney Point, Maryland, was approved by the USCG for signing five celestial assessments. After we completed the theory in class, we boarded the *Osprey* training ship and went out on the Chesapeake Bay to complete the assessments. It was a great class, and all the students got to complete their assessments, which were signed by the instructor. Every student passed the class and the assessments after three weeks, having never taken a celestial fix (position) before. The OS to AB assessments can be signed off in a classroom setting, but it is preferred to get them signed onboard ship. Some assessments are quite difficult to get signed in a classroom setting; celestial assessments being the toughest, in my opinion. Any you cannot get signed in the classroom, can be signed onboard ship with the appropriate equipment.

The completion of the RFPNW (OS to AB) class may reduce your sea time requirement for the STCW certification. If you already have four months of sea time as an OS, you should take the class. You might not have to go back to get the entire six months. This does not relieve you of getting all the sea service for your

AB requirement. The definition from policy letter [14-02] below defines what can be substituted for sea time.

"Applicants for the STCW certification must provide evidence of:

A. Either six months of approved, seagoing service that includes training and experience associated with navigational watchkeeping functions and involves duties carried out under the direct supervision of the master, officer in charge of the navigational watch or qualified ratings; or

B. Satisfactory completion of a course approved or accepted as "special training" required by the STCW plus a period of approved seagoing service. The length of the period of approved seagoing service will be specified as part of the course's approval and will not be less than two months; and

C. Evidence that the applicant meets the standards of 46 CFR 12.05-5 with regard to eye sight, color vision, and hearing."

Note that B. says that the sea service will not be less than two months. So you know if you take the class and get the certificate and assessments, you will have to have at least two months of sea time to get your STCW ratings certificate.

Again, make sure the school is approved to sign assessments. After you read this book, you will know more about USCG policy than some of the administrators at the schools. When you are signing up for the class and need the practical assessments signed, ask the instructor if the class is approved to do so. If not, you might end up taking the class and getting the certificate upon completion only to then realize they cannot sign the assessments because they were not approved.

A good friend of mine getting his third mate's license was told by a school that they would "take care of everything" regarding the new third mate classes. He asked about the assessments he needed to get signed, and the school assured him that his assessments would be signed. After enrolling in the school and paying the tuition, he found out after a couple of classes that the school was not approved to sign certain assessments. His plan of getting everything done at this school went out the window and his frustration grew. He ended up walking out of the school, leaving partially paid tuition that the school would not refund, and his assessments were still not completed. This prolonged the license process and he lost an opportunity to ship as a third mate with a company that was waiting for him to get his license.

Lessons learned from this example: Companies will help you get your license and promote you to third mate if you show you are competent and capable during your time there. Unfortunately, they will not wait forever. Do not let this happen.

You can imagine the frustration my friend felt after being told that "everything would be taken care of," only to find that so much was not. The schools are getting better at having all their classes approved for certificates and assessment signing. The USCG Web site lists the approved school and the assessments each class is approved to sign. They are listed by control number or STCW table number. I cannot stress this enough: Make sure the school is approved by the USCG to do what you want it to do regarding certificates and assessments. Ask school officials upfront before enrolling if there are any gaps or if the school is not approved to sign all the assessments you need. Remember that they might not have the equipment to complete all the assessments and cannot sign all of the assessments until they do.

STCW Competency

All assessments fall under a broad STCW competency subject. The "Function" of the assessment is in what manner the assessment is used onboard ship. An example of a function is "Navigation at the Operational Level." The "Competence" section details with which part of the "Function" subject the assessment deals. For example, "Plan and Conduct a Passage and Determine a Position."

Narrowing it down to what is the exact subject for each assessment is called the KUP or Knowledge, Understanding, and Proficiency. This section outlines on what subject, like Celestial Navigation, ARPA, Navigational Charts, etc., the mariner will focus. The "Task" is what the mariner is asked to do. For example: Task: Adjust a sextant. There are many different adjustments to a sextant and different methods and orders to do so. To relieve the interpretation, each assessment has "performance conditions, performance behaviors, and performance standards."

The performance condition explains the task in detail so no interpretation is left and there isn't any confusion between the assessor and the mariner being assessed. The performance behavior is the result of the performance condition.

Last is the performance standards, which are the guidelines by which the assessment is completed and the amount of error allowed for the assessment to pass. For example, control sheet OICNW 1-1A, "Task: Adjust a sextant. Performance condition: On a ship underway, given a standard marine sextant with a perpendicularity error, side error, parallelism error, and collimation error, totaling no more than two minutes and a clear horizon or sharply defined cloud. Performance behavior: Remove the adjustable sextant error. Performance standard: The errors were removed in the following order a. Perpendicularity b. Side c. Parallelism d. Collimation and the remaining index error was less than 0.5 minutes of arc."

This is as detailed as the assessments need to be. I wanted to cover it once, so the mariner understands the subject matter and guidelines in which to complete each assessment. These are still new, but you usually can run across somebody onboard the ship or in the classroom who has had to get them signed or has had to sign as an assessor. That makes it easier to explain. Also, I wanted to confirm that there is little interpretation left so the mariner and assessor can agree to the tasks at hand.

Once, I had an instructor at Maritime Professional Training in Ft. Lauderdale sign an assessment for me during my shiphandling and steering control course, and he and I interpreted key commands differently. The task was to change the ship's course 45 degrees, and the "Performance standards" were to complete the course change within +/- 5 degrees. The instructor interpreted the course change task to be done with only one rudder command, and no counter rudder to steady on course, like a traditional turn. I voiced my opinion that the course change should be made with as many rudder commands as needed to steady the vessel on its new heading safely and efficiently. The instructor argued that if the assessment was to be done that way, the control sheet would have explained that in the "Performance conditions and behaviors" on the control sheet. The control sheet had simply stated that the ship's course had to be changed 45 degrees, and had no details regarding helm and rudder commands.

This is an example of a gray area in the explanation of each assessment that can still exist. If you find yourself disagreeing with the assessor or instructor, keep your head up and try to empathize with the assessor's opinion. Explain your interpretation of the specific task and the reason behind your interpretation. I explained to my instructor that I understood that the assessment could be interpreted the way he did, using only one rudder command to learn the discipline and familiarity of the vessel for a 45 degree course change. But I argued that using multiple rudder commands, including counter rudder, seemed more along the lines of what a ship would do in a real circumstance. Having to change course 45 degrees, there is less room for deviation from the ordered course using multiple rudder commands.

He took my interpretation into consideration and agreed with it. Nonetheless, he made me fulfill the assessment by using only one rudder command. It took more than a couple of tries to land a ship exactly on a 45 degree course change using only one rudder command. I finally completed it, and he signed the assessment.

Follow the assessor's instruction even though it might go against your opinion. The signature is what you are after. If you can do it the way you interpret the task, you should be able to figure out how to do the assessor's interpretation of it. Arguing only pushes you further away from your signatures.

Filling Out the Assessment

Your name goes on the "Mariner" line. Your social security number goes on the "SSN" line. The rest has the assessor's information: their name, license number, MMD number, signature, rank, date, ship or training center. I recommend filling out all the information you can on the assessments sheets. This speeds up the process for the assessor, who has already put in a lot of time teaching you the subject matter. Make their signature the easiest part. Get their license information and fill out everything but the signature. That way, all they have to do is sign their name. If you are doing the assessments through a school, the instructor usually has them filled out already. If not, keep it in mind come signing time.

Being the Assessor

For the assessor doing the teaching, grading, or signing, a manual is available that explains how to serve as an assessor while onboard ship. It should be read and signed by the officer or instructor doing the evaluations. Usually classroom instructors have already done this, but it doesn't hurt to ask. Onboard the ships you will find that few know what you are talking about when you ask them to sign your assessments. It is important for you to always have a copy of the assessor's manual. I recommend that after the assessor reads the manual, have the assessor sign the manual itself—date, initials, anything to prove to the USCG that you did as much as could be done to follow its instruction.

"Where do I find this stupid manual?" you may ask. It is called *Conducting Mariner Assessments: A Practical Manual for Assessors.* The original thirteen-page manual is available at: http://www.uscg.mil/hq/g-m/marpers/pag/assessors.pdf.

I have included the manual at the end of this chapter. Read it to understand what could be expected of you at testing time. Better yet, print it from the USCG Web site and keep it with the rest of your assessments. Keep it in your assessment binder and have it available to give to someone at any time. The manual does not feature a signature line, so even if the assessor reads it, you have no proof they have done so. Again, I recommend asking if the assessing officer would initial the document if you are getting the assessments done on board ship.

It is important to know that the assessing officer's signature validates the assessment only at the time of the assessment. When the candidate has successfully completed an assessment and it is signed, that means that the mariner was found competent at the subject or task at the time of the assessment. From then on, the responsibility falls solely on the candidate for that task or subject, which means that the assessor is not responsible.

Some of the officers I met on board (especially new second mates) were terrified to sign anything, and some still won't. They feel that if they signed an AB's assessments, and that AB becomes a mate and has a serious marine incident, like a grounding or collision, the USCG will investigate the assessments on file for the person who signed that mate, and fine the assessor or question the assessor's license.

If this were the case, do you think anyone would sign any assessment? I know I wouldn't. It is a misunderstanding and hurdle that hawsepipers and assessors must get over. If they still do not believe you and refuse to sign anything (and there will be plenty of them), go to another officer. The idea behind the assessments is that the student is found competent at the time of the evaluation. Usually the chief mate works the best. If they are a watchstander, shadow their watch once a day. If not, you still have the captain, and second mate, sometimes a cargo mate. Start humbly, and always explain what you are trying to do. If everything fails, give the assessor this book and have them read this chapter.

Some of the maritime schools offer a course on becoming a shipboard assessor. It is not mandatory...yet.

Coast Guard Assessment Manual
Conducting Mariner Assessments
A Practical Manual For Assessors

This Manual is intended for assessors preparing to conduct over-the-shoulder assessments of mariner proficiencies. It was originally written to support shipboard trials of assessments by regular ship officers, who had little other training or preparation in assessment and little time to prepare.

The version here has been substantially revised to benefit from lessons learned during the trials. The ship officers and researchers performing the trials concluded that a short, concise manual provides adequate preparation, provided it is accompanied by an assessment "package" prepared for their ship's procedures and equipment. The Manual will also be useful for others who are responsible for assessment, including instructors at training facilities or academies. It is appropriate for inclusion in train-the-trainer or train-the-assessor courses.

CHAPTER 2 – TABLE OF CONTENTS

LIST OF FIGURES

LIST OF TABLES

INTRODUCTION

The STCW Challenge

Recent enactment of the Seafarers' Training, Certification and Watchkeeping (STCW) Code by the IMO has led to new requirements in conducting assessments of mariner proficiency. The STCW Code identifies a broad set of proficiency areas comprised of skills, knowledge, and abilities. It further directs maritime industries in its member nations to assess mariner proficiency in selected areas on the basis of practical demonstration. Assessors will be responsible for administering assessments to mariners and ensuring that valid and reliable results are obtained.

The Role of the Assessor

As an assessor, you will be responsible for assessing the ability of candidates to perform a task, duty, or responsibility properly. You will use established criteria and professional judgment to determine whether the candidate has demonstrated an acceptable level of proficiency. You will use assessment procedures that have been carefully developed, reviewed, and approved prior to the assessment. You should personally observe the mariner's performance and determine the outcome of the assessment.

An assessor should hold the level of license, endorsement, or professional credential required for the proficiency being assessed. In addition, the assessor should review the assessment materials and receive a basic introduction to techniques and issues associated with assessing mariner proficiency through practical demonstration.

Purpose of Manual

The purpose of this manual is to provide assessors with guidelines for conducting valid and reliable mariner assessments based on practical demonstration. This manual is not intended to provide comprehensive instruction in the full range of assessment issues. Rather, it is intended as a focused introduction and reference to selected factors that affect validity (job criticality) and reliability (consistency) while conducting such assessments. The process and guidance presented in this manual conform to international standards and domestic regulations, especially the IMO's STCW Code and the U.S. Coast Guard's Navigation and Vessel Inspection Circulars (NVICs) that address implementation of the STCW Code within the United States. The reference section of this manual lists specific STCW documents, applicable NV-ICs, and other source documents that can be referred to for more detailed guidance in developing and conducting mariner assessments based on practical demonstration.

Components of an Assessment Procedure

Any assessment procedure that is designed to meet IMO and U.S. Coast Guard requirements for practical demonstration of mariner proficiency will typically be comprised of several common components: assessment objectives, assessment conditions, performance measures, performance standards, and scoring procedures. As an assessor, you should familiarize yourself with these components, referring to the specific assessment procedures you will be using. When conducting an assessment, you will evaluate a candidate's ability to meet pre-defined assessment objectives. These objectives can be derived from the STCW Code and U.S. regulations, as well as technical manuals, job instructions, textbooks, and task analyses. Each assessment objective consists of one or more separate actions. An example assessment objective from a Lookout assessment is "describe lookout duties and responsibilities." As part of this objective, the candidate must demonstrate knowledge of the procedures for reporting sightings, including identifying and describing the procedure and reporting all relevant information. An example objective from a Prepare Main Engine for Operation assessment is "perform engine auxiliaries pre-start checks."

To meet this objective, one action the candidate must perform is to determine the status of the main engine controls and ensure that they are appropriate for starting the main engine. The candidate's performance on the stated assessment objectives will be evaluated under various assessment conditions. Conditions for the Lookout assessment, for example, include the presence of appropriate targets to be sighted, clear visibility during daylight and at night, and restricted visibility. The assessment conditions will be explicitly defined in the assessment procedures. Each assessment objective will have one or more corresponding sets of performance measures and performance standards.

Performance measures include observation and recording of specific mariner actions, or the outcome of those actions. Table 2-1 below provides a sample of mariner actions, performance measures, performance standards, and a scoring checklist from a Helmsman assessment procedure. It shows three of the five actions for the assessment objective "Demonstrates use of magnetic and gyro compasses in open waters." The first performance measure in this table is "Report of compass comparison," which is measured when assessing the action "Compare and report course by gyro and magnetic compass after a course change." Here, the assessor is required to record the mariner's report of the compass comparison, then apply the corresponding performance standard.

Performance standards specify the level of performance that is considered an acceptable or target level. Continuing with the example in the first row of Table 2-1, there are two performance standards that are to be applied in scoring the corresponding performance measure. In this case, the mariner is required to both: (1) make a report after the course change and (2) provide a reported magnetic reading that is +/- 2 degrees of actual.

Scoring procedures are used in scoring individual actions, as well as sets of scores to determine the outcome of performance assessments. Both of these types of scoring procedures should be explicitly defined in the assessment procedures. Pass/fail is the most common scoring procedure for individual actions. In this case, a candidate obtains a passing score for an action by passing all performance standards corresponding to that action. Scoring procedures applied to sets of multiple scores will most commonly be based on some range of acceptable scores. However, assessments often involve critical objectives that must be passed or the candidate fails the entire assessment. For example, a candidate undertaking an assessment of his ability to start the main engine must be able to correctly place the emergency stop valve in the run position. This action is essential to safe job performance, so a candidate must be able to perform it to pass the assessment.

Table 2-1. Example of Actions, Performance Measures, and Performance

Standards from the Helmsman Assessment

Action Performance

Measure

Performance Standard Score

Compare and report course by gyro and magnetic compass after a course change. Report of compass comparison.

Performance meets all standards:
☐ Report after course change.
☐ Reported magnetic reading to be +/- 2 degrees of actual.
☐ Pass
☐ Fail
☐ N/A

Compare and report course by gyro and magnetic compass periodically. Report of compass comparison.

Performance meets all standards:
☐ Report at the time interval specified in the standing orders or company policy.

Comparison of gyro and magnetic compass to be unprompted by assessor/watch officer if consistent with company procedures.
☐ Reported magnetic reading to be +/- 2 degrees of actual.
☐ Pass
☐ Fail
☐ N/A

Steer by magnetic compass in moderate weather. Maintain a steady course.

Course to be maintained at +/- 5 degrees of ordered course for 30 minutes, relying solely upon the magnetic compass. In adverse winds or current, allowance can be made for a less stringent standard.
☐ Pass
☐ Fail
☐ N/A

Overview of the Assessment Process

You should follow the same basic series of five steps in conducting an assessment, even if you are conducting assessments of a number of mariner proficiencies. The first step is to prepare for the assessment by reviewing and ensuring the required assessment conditions and scheduling the assessment at an appropriate time (e.g., at night for certain Lookout objectives). The second step is to brief the candidate before the assessment. This involves verifying the candidate's readiness to undertake the assessment and then briefing the candidate on the assessment objectives, measures, standards, and scoring. The third step involves observing the candidate's performance during the assessment and recording the results. For the fourth step, the assessment outcome is determined by scoring each performance measure and tallying the scores across objectives. The fifth and final step is to debrief the candidate following the assessment. Figure 2-1 depicts the steps involved in conducting an assessment.

Figure 2-1. Steps involved in conducting mariner assessments based on practical demonstration.

The remainder of this manual consists of guidelines for conducting mariner assessments. The guidelines are organized around the five steps involved in conducting mariner assessments. At each step, guidance is provided regarding factors to consider in preparing for and conducting assessments, followed by a general checklist of issues to consider.

Guidelines for Conducting Mariner Assessments

As an assessor, you should always strive to conduct valid and reliable assessments. An assessment is valid when it accurately measures the job-critical knowledge, skills, and abilities required for proficient job performance. An assessment is reliable when it consistently obtains the same results across mariners with comparable skills.

How do you know if you are prepared to conduct a valid assessment that will accurately measure the job-critical knowledge, skills, and abilities required for proficient job performance?

Your assessment will be valid if the conditions of assessment reasonably reflect arepresentative range of working conditions and requirements. Some questions you shouldconsider in determining whether you are prepared to conduct a valid assessment are listed below.

☐ Will the assessment be conducted under realistic working conditions that adequately assess the mariner's abilities to perform his or her duties on the job?

☐ Will the mariner be required to demonstrate the skills and knowledge that are identified in the assessment as critical to proficiency?

☐ Will the mariner be required to rely on his or her own skills and knowledge?

Step 1: Prepare for the assessment

Step 2: Brief the candidate before the assessment

Step 3: Observe the candidate's performance

Step 4: Determine the assessment outcome

Step 5: Debrief the candidate

How do you know if you are prepared to conduct a reliable assessment that will consistently obtain the same results across mariners with comparable skills?

Your assessment will be reliable if you carefully follow prescribed assessment procedures that are designed to ensure consistent results from one assessment to the next. Some questions you should consider in determining whether you are prepared to conduct a reliable assessment are listed below.

☐ Have you reviewed the instructions in the assessment package to ensure that you are prepared to carefully follow prescribed assessment procedures?

☐ Will you provide the candidate with a complete set of instructions and answer any appropriate questions that he or she may have?

☐ Are you prepared to accurately observe and record all mariner performance, as instructed in the assessment package?

Step 1: Prepare for the Assessment

Ideally, you should begin preparing for an assessment several days before it is scheduled. The first activity is to coordinate the assessment with the candidate(s) to ensure that they are properly prepared and qualified to take part in the assessment. Each assessment procedure should specify candidate prerequisites for assessment, in terms of prior training, experience, licenses, and successful completion of other related assessments. If these are absent, they should be discussed and established by those responsible for assessment in your organization. You should verify that a candidate meets all prerequisites for an assessment. In addition, you should determine that a candidate is scheduled to be onboard for an adequate period of time to complete the assessment, which will range from an hour to days or weeks, depending upon the specific assessment procedures.

The second activity involved in preparing for the assessment is to consider and plan for the required conditions. Carefully read the assessment conditions listed in the assessment procedures. Prior to conducting an onboard assessment, check your passage plan to determine when the required conditions might be present. Plan to schedule your assessment to match the availability of these conditions, if possible. Common conditions that can often be planned for in advance are being underway at sea, maneuvering in restricted waters, or being moored. Other conditions, such as restricted visibility or heavy seas, cannot be planned for in advance and can only be taken advantage of when the conditions arise. When you have prepared a schedule, inform the candidate(s), the relevant watch officer(s), and other personnel of the date and time(s) of the assessment so that they can plan their activities accordingly. The third preparatory activity is to check all equipment required for the assessment and ensure that it is operational and available. The assessment procedures should specify the equipment required to assess a particular proficiency. If an engineering assessment involves checking equipment status, make sure you know the normal range for each variable and record this information so that you can refer to it during the assessment. As part of your check of equipment, you should also review all applicable safety precautions and procedures to ensure full adherence to them.

General Checklist for Assessment Preparation
☐ Gather and review all assessment materials.
☐ Verify that the candidate meets the assessment prerequisites.
☐ Check the candidate's duty schedule.
☐ Ensure that the appropriate conditions will be present for the assessment.
☐ Schedule the assessment and inform all affected personnel.
☐ Prepare the assessment area(s).
☐ Prepare and arrange the necessary equipment, and ensure that it is operational.
☐ Determine the necessary safety precautions.

Step 2: Brief the Candidate before the Assessment
The pre-assessment briefing should take place at least one day prior to the assessment (earlier if at all possible). This will help both you and the candidate to be well prepared for the as-

sessment. During this briefing, you should provide the candidate with a copy of the Candidate Instructions and Assessment Control Sheet. The Candidate Instructions are instructions prepared especially for the candidate, focusing on the issues that will be of concern to that individual. The Assessment Control Sheet summarizes the assessment objectives and all of the actions required for each objective. It is also the document on which you will record the candidate's final scores for each objective.

Begin the briefing with a discussion of the candidate's prior experience, training, and qualifications. At this time, you should verify that this candidate is both qualified and willing to undertake the assessment. If you both agree the candidate is ready for the assessment, then continue with the assessment process. If not, arrange for additional on-the-job or simulator training and set a date for another review of the candidate's qualifications.

Review the conditions of the assessment with the candidate. Specifically, discuss the different operational conditions under which assessment will occur. You should also discuss the period of assessment. Some assessments can be completed in a single, relatively brief period of time. Other assessments require repeated observation, taking advantage of available conditions, such as restricted visibility, as they occur.

Safety is of paramount concern during the assessment. Because of this, you should remind the candidate that it is permissible to ask questions during the assessment. This can help to reduce the risk of an unsafe act during the course of the assessment. For all assessments, ensure that the candidate has the proper equipment to carry out the assessment. Inform the candidate that an assessment will be stopped at any time if you, the assessor, judge that safety conditions are being violated for any reason.

General Checklist for Briefing the Candidate before the Assessment

☐ Provide the candidate with copies of the Candidate Instructions and Assessment Control Sheet.
☐ Discuss the candidate's readiness for the assessment.
☐ Review the Candidate Instructions with the candidate and answer any questions.
☐ Discuss the desired outcome(s) and consequences of failing to perform part or all of the assessment.

☐ Advise the candidate of the conditions and schedule of the assessment.

☐ Review the circumstances under which the assessment will be terminated, due to safety concerns.

Step 3: Observe the Candidate's Performance

The third step in the assessment process is to observe the candidate's performance during the assessment. Remember that you must continuously observe the candidate. Throughout the assessment, require the candidate to adhere to standard procedures, except when assessment procedures require demonstration of knowledge or skills different from those standard procedures. For example, a company may use points to report sightings, but a candidate may also be asked to demonstrate knowledge of the relative bearing system as part of the Lookout assessment.

Specific assessment objectives, performance measures, performance standards, and scoring procedures will be included in each assessment. Your consistent application of these procedures will ensure that you conduct a valid and reliable assessment. However, adherence to these procedures may require some flexibility on your part. Specifically, in some cases you may be required to remember the performance of the candidate for some time before you are able to record and score his or her performance. In addition, there may be times during the assessment when you will need to ask the candidate what he or she is doing. You should try to limit your questions during the candidate's performance, so that you minimize the amount of coaching the candidate receives from you.

Typically, an assessment will include a number of questions regarding the candidate's knowledge of rules and procedures pertaining to the duties under assessment. In addition, there will commonly be a number of questions regarding the candidate's performance that must be asked for clarification. Generally, a good time to ask all of these questions is following the candidate's demonstration of practical skills. At this point, you can ask specific questions you have about the performance you observed and use these questions as introductions, when appropriate, to more general questions about knowledge and rules included as part of the assessment.

Remember that, in order to maintain assessment validity and reliability, candidates should be assessed on their ability to perform their job tasks and duties and to demonstrate their knowledge of job procedures and rules. Avoid training candidates to successfully complete an assessment rather than proficiently perform their job. Also avoid allowing candidates to observe assessments of other mariners when this will provide them with an unfair advantage during subsequent assessment.

Finally, it is important to remain constantly vigilant regarding operational effectiveness and safety. Assessments should be conducted only where they do not adversely affect the normal operation of the ship. In addition, assessments must be terminated whenever safety conditions are being violated.

General Checklist for Observing the Candidate's Performance

☐ If a safety violation occurs, terminate the assessment immediately.

☐ Ensure that the candidate can concentrate on the task at hand.

☐ Do not allow other crewmembers to interfere with the assessment.

☐ Ensure realistic assessment conditions with a normal working environment.

☐ Continuously observe the candidate during the assessment.

☐ Record the observed performance and apply the performance standards as soon as practical during the assessment.

☐ Require that standard procedures be adhered to, except when assessment procedures require demonstration of knowledge or skill different from these procedures.

☐ Avoid asking leading questions. Try to keep your questions fair but general in nature.

☐ Avoid giving the candidate unsolicited assistance, but respond to appropriate questions and provide appropriate equipment when required.

☐ Remain objective and maintain positive control of the operation at all times.

Step 4: Record Results and Determine Assessment Outcome

The fourth step in the assessment process is to determine the assessment outcome. To do this, record the candidate's performance on each Assessment Worksheet and then apply the scoring procedures specified in the assessment procedures. Remember that if the candidate incorrectly performs any of the critical, required actions, he or she automatically fails the entire assessment.

Finally, determine and document the outcome of the assessment, transferring the final results to the Assessment Control Sheet. You will probably have some additional paperwork requirements that have been specified by your organization. This will likely involve the maintenance of personnel records within your organization. In addition, upon successful completion of an assessment by a candidate, you will need to make the appropriate entries in the Training Record Book that has been adopted by your organization as a means of documenting fulfillment of the corresponding STCW requirements by the mariner.

General Checklist for Determining Assessment Outcome
- ☐ Record performance on the appropriate Assessment Worksheet.
- ☐ Adhere strictly to the prescribed performance standards and scoring procedure(s).
- ☐ Determine and document the outcome of the assessment, then transfer the final results to the Assessment Control Sheet.
- ☐ Attest to successful demonstration of tasks in the Training Record Book (TRB) or other record, as appropriate.

Step 5: Debrief the Candidate

The fifth and final step in the assessment process is to debrief the candidate as soon as possible after the assessment. During this debriefing, you should restate the assessment objectives and discuss the candidate's performance on each objective. A good strategy for beginning a debriefing is to review the candidate's positive accomplishments. The candidate will then likely be in a better frame of mind to hear any comments regarding areas needing improvement. If the candidate failed to demonstrate proficiency, you may work together with him or her to develop an improvement plan to prepare for reassessment. Conditions for conducting reassessments should be specified in the assessment procedure. If these are absent, they should be discussed and established by those responsible for assessment in your organization. Specific issues to consider are: (1) the period between initial assessment and reassessment, and (2) any changes in the performance standards and scoring procedures that are adopted for reassessment.

General Checklist for Debriefing the Candidate

☐ Debrief the candidate as soon as possible after the assessment.
☐ Restate the assessment objective(s).
☐ Focus on positive accomplishments first.
☐ Identify areas needing improvement.
☐ If the candidate failed to demonstrate proficiency, jointly develop an improvement plan to prepare for reassessment.

GLOSSARY

Assessor. Anyone who conducts an assessment or evaluation of an individual's proficiency. The term assessor is used in many discussions of STCW requirements, including the STCW Code and NVIC 4-97 on company roles and responsibilities. The term designated examiner is used for examiner in the United States implementing regulations.

Assessment. The process of evaluating whether an individual's performance meets established proficiency criteria. The terminology used for this process in the United States implementing regulations includes examination for knowledge, and an assessment based on practical demonstration, as witnessed by a designated examiner.

Assessment Conditions. The assessment conditions define the setting, tools, references, aids, and safety precautions that are required for an assessment of a candidate's proficiency.

Assessment Objectives. The goals for the performance-based assessment of proficiency based on the knowledge, skills, and abilities required by the job. A complete assessment objective description includes the required mariner performance, the conditions of assessment, and the standards of performance for successful accomplishment of the objective.

Assessment Procedures. The activities that are conducted in administering the assessment of a candidate's proficiency. The term assessment procedure can describe either the actions taken or the written instructions and activity descriptions that are used in conducting an assessment.

Designated Examiner. A person who has been trained or instructed in techniques of training or assessment and is otherwise qualified to administer performance assessment procedures. In practice, the designated examiner evaluates whether the candidate's performance meets established proficiency criteria to earn credit toward the license, document, or endorsement. Further details on the qualifications of designated examiner can be found in NVIC 6-97.

Duty. An ongoing responsibility within a job that usually requires the performance of multiple tasks (e.g., Officer in Charge of the Engineering Watch, Lookout, and Helmsman).

Evaluation Criteria. The evaluation criteria comprise the general standards of competence. In practice, the evaluation criteria are further defined on the basis of performance measures, performance standards, and proficiency criteria.

Job. An employment post consisting of a cluster of related work responsibilities and duties (e.g., Chief Engineer, Third Mate, Able-bodied Seaman). In the STCW Code, a job is further defined on the basis of licensure level (e.g., Officer in charge of a navigational watch on ships of 500 gross tonnage or more).

Knowledge. The learned concepts, cues, facts, rules, and procedures that are necessary for proficient performance of a task (e.g., knowledge of algebra, knowledge of the Navigation Rules, knowledge of procedures for starting the main engine).

Objective Measure. A measure that relies primarily upon measurement apparatus that can be calibrated to yield highly consistent and accurate measurement results.

Performance Measure. The procedures used for observing and recording mariner actions, or the outcome of those actions. Performance measures record either the process of performance or the product of performance.

Performance Standard. The standard established for individual performance measures.

Performance measures and performance standards are combined on the basis of scoring procedures to establish proficiency criteria for an assessment objective.

Proficiency. An individual's demonstrated ability to meet job performance requirements, as established on the basis of performance measures, performance standards, and proficiency criteria.

Proficiency Criteria. The scoring procedures and standards applied in determining the proficiency level of a candidate on the basis of performance measures and performance standards.

Qualified Instructor. According to the United States implementing regulations: "the person who has been trained or instructed in instructional techniques and is otherwise qualified to provide required training to candidates for licenses, documents, or endorsements." Further details on the qualifications of qualified instructors can be found in NVIC 6-97.

Reliability. The consistency of a measurement procedure. In the context of assessment, reliability can be generally defined as the consistency of the assessment outcome when applied under comparable conditions. Reliable assessments have well-defined assessment conditions, administration procedures, performance measures, performance standards, scoring procedures, and proficiency criteria. The reliability of an assessment establishes the maximum level of assessment validity possible. That is, an assessment cannot be any more valid than it is reliable.

Scoring Procedures. The defined procedures for combining individual performance measures and performance standards that are conducted in the application of proficiency criteria.

Skills and Abilities. The behaviors that must be applied in successful performance (e.g., typing skills, equipment fault-finding skills, navigation skills, shiphandling skills). Measurable and observable skills are those of interest in proficiency assessment.

Subjective Measure. A measure that relies primarily upon an assessor's direct observation and interpretation of mariner performance to determine the assessment outcome.

Task. A single, observable work assignment that is independent of other actions and supports successful job performance. A task must be observable, be a complete work assignment, have a specific beginning and end, and be measurable by its intended product or outcome.

Validity. The extent to which a measure represents what was intended to be measured. In the context of assessment, validity can be defined as the degree to which successful completion of an assessment accurately predicts successful performance on the job. The maximum validity of an assessment is established on the basis of its reliability. That is, an assessment cannot be any more valid than it is reliable.

REFERENCES

46 C.F.R. §97.27-5. (1997). Lookouts. *U.S. Code of Federal Regulations*. U.S. Coast Guard, U.S. Department of Transportation. Washington, DC: Office of the Federal Register.

Gagné, R., Briggs, L., & Wagner, W. (1992). Principles of instructional design (4th ed.). Fort Worth, Texas: Harcourt Brace College Publishers.

International Maritime Organization. (1995). International Convention on Standards of Training, Certification and Watchkeeping for Seafarers, 1978, as amended in 1995 (STCW Convention). London: Author. International Maritime Organization. (1996). Seafarer's Training, Certification, and Watchkeeping (STCW) Code. London: Author.

International Maritime Organization. (1998). Guidance on shipboard assessments of proficiency. (Marine Safety Committee Circular No. 853). London: Author.

McCallum, M. C., Forsythe, A. M., Barnes, A. E., Smith, M. W., Macaulay, J., Sandberg, G. R., Murphy, J., & Jackson, P. (2000). A Method for Developing Mariner Assessments (Report No. R&DC 202). Groton, CT: U.S. Coast Guard Research & Development Center.

United States Coast Guard. (1997). Guidance on Company Roles and Responsibilities under the 1995 Amendments to the International Convention on Standards of Training, Certification and Watchkeeping (STCW). Navigation and Vessel Inspection Circular No. 4-97 [Online].Available: http://www.uscg.mil/hq/g-m/nvic/4_97/n4-97.htm.

United States Coast Guard. (1997B). Guidance on qualified instructors and designated examiners. Navigation and Vessel Inspection Circular No. 6-97 [Online]. Available: http://www.uscg.mil/hq/g-m/nvic/6-97/n6-97/n7-97.htm.

United States Coast Guard. (1997C). Guidance on STCW quality standards systems (QSS) for merchant mariner courses or training programs. Navigation and Vessel Inspection Circular No.7-97 [Online]. Available: http://www.uscg.mil/hq/g-m/nvic/7-97/n7-97.htm.

United States Coast Guard. (1995). Guidelines for Organizations Offering Coast Guard Approved Courses. Navigation and Vessel Inspection Circular No.[5-95][X-98] [Online]. Available: http://www.uscg.mil/hq/g-m/nvic/5_95/n5-95.htm.

Chapter Seven
Financing for School

Taking the time to complete all the classes you need, learning each subject and passing the tests, or completing all the required assessments and additional company or union endorsements is hard enough. An equally daunting task is answering this big question: How do I pay for this?

If we return to that fantasy world I discussed in chapter one, someone would be paying you a good salary while you take the classes for free. However, the reality is, if you attend school full-time, you will not be able to work and earn money, and the classes are anything but free. That does not mean you cannot earn money another way while paying for classes. It is still a great sacrifice to climb the hawsepipe, but it is well worth it and can be done using little of your own money…really!

The realities of our present economy have made policymakers realize the importance of job training and to make funds available to those who want and need them.

American laborers are slowly being phased out of their professions due to lack of resources (no fish, no crab, no trees, no oil, no nothing), outsourcing (shipping the job to a three-year-old in Taiwan, who probably gets three cents a day and a slice of bread), or automation ("Sorry folks, you're being replaced by computerized robots. Have a great day!"). Whatever the case, American laborers are finding themselves in a pinch. Their profession might no longer exist, or the industry has shrunk so small that it no longer has room for everyone. In the 1990s politicians recognized the need for programs that involved worker retraining or training for advancement. In the maritime industry we have both.

For example, the Alaskan crabbing and fishing industry has declined to the extent that displaced fishermen throughout Washington and Oregon are wondering what to do. The days of heavy fishing and crabbing are over. The restrictions on fishing and crabbing are extreme. There is no longer the volume of fish and crab there used to be; consequently, it is very hard to make a living at it, unless you are one of the few to receive an allocated portion of the pot, which means a quota. To help crabbers transition from that line of work to another in the maritime industry, the government established the Displaced Alaskan Fisherman Program. The program provided funds to displaced fisherman for retraining in other professions, such as the merchant marines. Seagoing workers who found themselves without jobs in Alaska could qualify for training to get an STCW 95 certificate, AB, or limited tonnage license, to work in a related industry, such as the Alaskan Marine Highway (ferries).

Usually the schools the mariners attend are linked with these government programs, so if a student qualifies for the program, the school contacts the financial program's office to verify the student's eligibility and works with that office for tuition payment. The student pays nothing. The school must be approved to accept money from specific government programs, so it is important to ask the school whether they are approved for the program you qualify for; be it government retraining, scholarship, military, or any form of financial aid. Also, the award is based on whether you pass the class or not, so you do not want to fail the courses you take that is based on a grant, scholarship, or other aid. You usually have to pay back any money given for any course you fail. Know ahead of time how much each training course costs and how you are going to pay for it.

Like any free money, funding usually is limited for each individual and will expire if not used.

If you qualify, the Alaskan Displaced Fisherman's Program is great for the basics like STCW, AB, BST, Life Boatman, 100 ton/200 ton master, but when it comes to getting the Officer in Charge of a Navigational Watch, for mates 500 tons and above, it takes a lot more money and time. Classes like Basic Shiphandling can cost up to $3,500, and that is just a one-week class. To use the programs available to you, implement a matrix to maximize every cent.

First, look to your company or union for help. If you are reading this, you plan to become a mate and should be talking to these organizations already for what they offer in the form of financial aid. Some unions, for example, have their own training schools, where you can take classes, granted you satisfy their requirements. The first question you should ask an employer or union is,

"Do you have an upgrading program?" or "Do you have financial assistance to upgrade?"

If the answer to either is yes, the next question is "What do I have to do to qualify?"

When I sailed for SIU as an AB, I didn't care about the job or the money or the benefits; I wanted to know about the schooling. The patrolman in Tacoma, Washington, was very informative and helpful. He said they had their own school in Piney Point, Maryland, and as an AB, I could go to school at no charge as long as I sailed 120 days each year. So, for four months, I sailed as an AB. Upon completion, I flew to Piney Point and started my upgrading classes. I alternated work and school until I had taken every class Piney Point had to offer. It was well worth it.

Not all unions and companies have that availability, so make sure the one you are joining has the resources you need, because I will tell you this now: It is so much easier getting your mate's license when the company or union you work for pays for the schooling. This is the biggest selling point when accepting a job. It doesn't matter what the AB work is like, it is a means to an end when it comes to your training. So many mariners try to get the best paying AB job, or the best AB duty. Your task is to look past your AB time and think about your license. When I sailed as AB, I was on a ship that had, comparatively, a terrible union contract. The pay was below the standard contracts other ships' ABs were making. It didn't matter to me. I needed the sea time to qualify for school, so that is what I did. As a second mate sailing for Matson now, making three times what I was making as an AB, I look back on those AB days and ask myself if it was worth it. Guess what my answer is?

If you work for a company instead of a union, they will usually do it differently. Most of the time companies will reimburse some, or all, of the money for classes. Again, you have to qualify for the money by whatever requirements the company asks for, usually sailing time and successful completion of courses.

When I worked for ChevronTexaco as an AB, the policy was that the company would pay up to 75 percent of all tuition upon qualification. I know that the cost for the whole program, starting from scratch, can be around $20,000 to $26,000 dollars. That is a lot of money. Even having to pay 25 percent of that is a large bill, but think about having to pay for all of it. Like I said, companies usually require appropriate sea time with that company, and a successful completion of any course. To ensure that, they usually reimburse mariners after they take the class and not before, or pay the school directly after the course is done. Also, a company or union could have the mariner sign a letter of future commitment for their investment in your program.

After getting all my classes from SIU at Piney Point, I still needed additional classes to get my third mate's license. I researched other ways to get money for the rest of my classes. I found a wonderful program called WorkSource. This is part of the displaced workers program and is open to any person who qualifies. The program insists on three basic principals:

1. The industry you are in has no jobs or is shrinking.
2. The training needed is required for advancement or employment in a different field.
3. Jobs are available in the new industry you will be qualified to work in when the training is completed.

Putting it specifically for the mariner, there is no work now, the mariner has to take these classes to get their license, and when they do, they can get a job.

WorkSource is a government program that is segregated into counties. Whichever county you reside in, the money you receive will come from that county's pool. The reason this is important to you is how many people are in that county. I grew up in Seattle, Washington, which is a beautiful place, but growing as fast as it takes a fat man to slide down a greased fire pole. The main county for Seattle is King County. The ratio of people to money in a metropolitan area is obviously skewed. I walked into a throng of out-of-work people trying to apply for the training money that was quickly running out.

Another big hurdle I faced was explaining the industry I was in. They have no category for merchant mariners except marine engineer. I said that was close enough, but recommended they create a category for merchant mariner.

After that, I had to explain STCW 95, the license scheme, working on a ship, the whole thing. As you can imagine this did not get me very far. When the nice lady helping me said, "I don't think we can help you," I realized this was her canned response, which really meant, "I don't understand what you do and don't know how to help you."

I inquired further as to how the money was distributed. She told me it was by residence and county, so whichever county you lived in, that was the place to go (counties with large populations usually have more than one office). I was living in the beautiful Norwegian town of Poulsbo, Washington, in Kitsap County. I called the Kitsap County WorkSource, and the WorkSource office knew much more about the industry than King county did.

My reflection upon the difference between the Seattle (King) and Silverdale (Kitsap) offices was really the amount of people that lived in that county, how many of them are from the merchant marines or related industries, and how many people each office deals with per day.

I set up an appointment with one of the advisors and started from the beginning, again. After an in-depth conversation about the maritime industry, what is happening to it regarding the shrinking U.S. merchant fleet, and what I needed to obtain my license for a better job, the advisor was understanding of my situation and pretty happy to help me.

What he told me is that most folks do not know what to do after being displaced. The search for a new career and training is a huge task and WorkSource tries to help as much as they can, not only with money for training, but workshops on résumé building, job searches, computer skills, and more. WorkSource gets its money from the government according to how useful it can be to the people they retrain. If they allocate money for training and the workers don't pass the classes, drop out, or do not get a job after it is done, the government pulls the funding as a waste of taxpayers' dollars.

WorkSource looks for confident people who have the drive to get ahead and know what they want. Needless to say, you will be a welcome sight in the office when you come in and know exactly what you want and what they need from you. For them, you are one of the best clients they can have.

After our conversation, the advisor told me money was available and he needed the information regarding the lack of work, requirements of training, and proof of employment when the training is completed.

Saying it and actually doing it are two different things. Many companies and unions will not write a letter saying that there is no work— especially a union. If they write a letter saying they do not have work, they are shooting themselves in the foot because no one will join their union and pay dues. When I tried to get SIU to write a letter saying they did not have work, they would not do it and said they would get me a job, no problem.

Being a previous member, I understood their position and even explained why I needed the letter, but they still would not provide it. Their job was to find ABs work. If they state in writing that there aren't any jobs, they are failing the union members and dues-payers. If you worked for a company that had to let you go for economic reasons, that company might write you a letter stating that a lack of work or the work is seasonal. If a company, as opposed to a union, does not have any work, it is different and it might be easier to obtain this letter from a company. The most important thing is explanation. Employers obviously want to know why you need a letter like this. Explain that it is for educational purposes. You are trying to advance your career, and employers need to know that.

If anybody asks you what you are doing, you should; simply state: "I am upgrading my merchant mariner's document (or license) to third mate unlimited (or applicable license) and need to take the required classes. When the classes are completed I will be able to work in a capacity in which my advancement will be worth the time and money spent to get my new license."

To apply to WorkSource, go to a search engine like Yahoo or Google and type "WorkSource" and then your state of residence, like "Washington" in the text box, and click "Search." The WorkSource Web site for your area should pop up. Click on it and get the contact information for the office closest to you. I recommend not spending too much time filling out stuff via the Web, unless they are unable to see you soon at the office. Doing things in person gets more done, especially when it comes to getting free money.

Make an appointment to talk with an advisor and work with them to get the money you need. I wrote a letter to my advisor, which he forwarded with my package to get approval for me. I do not know if your advisor will ask you to write this letter, but it should be a chronological document of what it is necessary for you to upgrade and why you are doing it. The important points to stress are lack of work in your current position, required training by the Coast Guard, and job openings at the end of training.

This will take some research and phone calls to unions and companies for proof of licensed mate's jobs available, and lack of work from your union or company. Look online at the employment opportunities and copy those Web sites into a document about job opportunities as third mate. Remember, this is for your training and nothing else. Here is the letter I wrote. It wasn't perfect, but it worked.

November 7, 2003
To: WorkSource
1300 Sylvan Way
Bremerton, WA 98310
From: Leonard Lambert
216 NE Goldenchain Ct.
Poulsbo, WA 98370

To Whom It May Concern:

I am a merchant mariner who has been working in the capacity of able-bodied seaman (AB) on unlimited class container ships as well as a licensed mate onboard smaller vessels (1600 gross tons and below). I have nine years' experience with different companies dating back to 1991.

Recently, the employment in my field has greatly been reduced. As an able-bodied seaman I belonged to the Seafarers International Union and, unfortunately, they do not have employment for a person of my seniority (C book). My deck officer positions on the smaller, non-union vessels have gone away as well. The jobs for my industry, for one reason or another, simply are not as abundant as they once were.

This has led me to investigate a raise-in-grade for my merchant mariner's license from a 1,600 ton near-coastal mate, to a third mate unlimited ton oceans, which would allow me to work as an officer onboard many different vessels, including commercial, state ferries, oil tankers, military, international, and cruise ships. My research confirmed that any person wanting to become an unlimited tonnage officer must go through a rigorous training program and have a certain amount of time onboard vessels to qualify. These rules are set by the U.S. Coast Guard, as they are the governing body for my industry. As I knew the road would be long, I called some companies to make sure that there were jobs available once I completed all the training and testing. A major officers' union, American Maritime Officers Union (AMO), based in Dania, Florida, said since there is so much training involved now, there is a lack of officers because fewer and fewer people can take the time, spend the money, or comprehend all the training subjects. There is a need for unlimited third mates.

I have the required sea service, and have been taking many training classes, but have fallen short due to lack of money, which is why I am writing this letter. I have attached the list of all classes required, their respective dates and costs. I hope to continue my training to get the job I want and I look forward to a positive response.

Sincerely,
Leonard W. Lambert

This letter was attached with a class list, policy letter [01-02] stating the requirements, and a document of Web sites offering job opportunities to third mates.

The document that requires you to take these classes to get your license is the Coast Guard Policy letter [01-02], which states the requirements of training. Print a copy of the policy letter and put it with the rest of the info for WorkSource.

Solicit aid from anybody— school instructors, your company or union—to state that third-mate jobs will be available when the training is complete:.

After you have been approved, WorkSource deals with the training schools themselves. The office will notify you of how much you are allotted and how much time you have to spend it. This should coincide with your schedule of classes, which means do not get approved and go back to work, losing the money because too much time has elapsed. The money has time limits. Make sure you have a class schedule and are ready to go when the money comes in. Keep in contact with your WorkSource advisor and school administration along the way.

Each time I had a class I called my advisor and told them the dates, length, cost, school, and subject. He confirmed with the school and waited for my certificate. When I completed the class, I faxed a copy of the certificate to his office, and the school got paid through WorkSource. Let me reiterate, you will not see a dime of this money. This money is for training only and goes directly to the school from WorkSource. You just attend and pass the classes.

Keep track of the money spent, and when it is gone that's it. It is a one-time deal.

WorkSource is not need-based and does not require you to be poor to use it. The requirements are strictly on a training-need basis. If you satisfy the objectives talked about earlier, you should get money. I received about $3,500 from WorkSource, which paid for all but two of the remaining classes I needed. After I had my license in hand and totaled my expenses, I ended up spending only $6,000 of my own money, as opposed to the $26,000 needed.

Of course, while WorkSource, or any other financial program, is paying for your school, you are not making any money while attending classes. This is where programs like unemployment and student financial aid can really help. Whichever state you are from, you should qualify for unemployment benefits while training for a job.

First of all, be upfront with unemployment. You are not sneaking the money away from them by going to school and not looking for a job. Merchant mariners have been taking unemployment for years while not on a ship. This is nothing new. What gets confusing sometimes is which unemployment you should be using and what it is for. The best way to know is to start with your state of residence. They should tell you whether you need to file in another state and the contact number as well. Do not lie about training. Qualified programs within unemployment allow you to go to school for a job while getting benefits. I was living in Seattle but taking Maryland unemployment, because that is where the company I worked for was located. I had to go through a rigorous question and answer period with a Maryland representative from their unemployment office regarding my training. I had all the answers. To make sure I wasn't trying to pull a fast one, the representative said to go ahead and file each week, but to let them know if I was training or not. I got a weekly check from unemployment while WorkSource paid for my school. It was a nice deal. I owe my license and my current job to these government programs because without them, I couldn't have done it.

WorkSource has the information on unemployment benefits and might list benefits that I have not listed. Things are always changing. Ask as many questions and jump through all the hoops because it is worth it. Ask your company or union about all the benefits available to you while you take classes. There could be additional living wages paid to you while going to class, financial scholarships for mariners who qualify, reimbursement of classes taken in other maritime schools, classes provided by the company or ship onboard, etc. Mariners will never know what is available to them if they don't ask. State-funded grants and scholarships might be applicable. I know of a couple maritime schools that merged with community colleges, or are a part of an existing community college, which offer financial aid to students upon qualifying, just like a regular college. Imagine getting a WorkSource grant, unemployment benefits and scholastic financial aid while upgrading your license. You probably wouldn't have to pay a dime. The other students will ask you the same question they asked me, "How'd you do that?"

Make sure your financial matrix complies with the regulations. You can try to be sneaky and claim money that you do not qualify for and you might not get caught. But if you are, you will have to pay it back, usually with an additional fine or interest, and getting things done in the future will be a lot harder. Tell the truth about what you are doing. I believe hawsepiping is a righteous path, and these financial programs have been put in place for people like us trying to get a better job so we can have a better life.

Veterans should ask every question possible about military experience. Many merchant marine vessels work closely with the government and military. Veterans' experience can play a huge role in getting a MMD or license, and government programs are available to veterans for training, like the GI Bill or military college funds. I include more information on this in chapter nine.

Chapter Eight
They Are Finally Going to Let You Test

The money has been spent, the brain is in fizzle mode, and you are a walking encyclopedia of nautical terms and CFRs. You are ready to apply for your license. Before STCW 95, there was a voluntary prep class for mates, which ran about two to three months and covered all the subjects on the USCG exam. STCW 95 took those subjects and made separate classes for them, spreading out the prep class and requiring mariners to study each subject in depth, pass an exam on each subject, and obtain a Coast Guard STCW 95 certificate, along with demonstrating practical assessments for each subject. Putting it another way, the prep class is now more intense and it is required.

As a result, mariners should be ready to test after completion of all the classes. That was your study time. Now, the hard part is cramming it all in for your 3.5 day hell week of exams at the friendly Coast Guard REC. Don't worry, if you passed all the classes and assessments, you can pass the test and get your license.

The USCG application and evaluation process has problems. Here is the scenario: you have taken all your classes and are ready to submit your application to the USCG. (Remember, you cannot apply until all certificates, assessments and requirements have been met.) You are ready to test. The USCG takes your application, certificates, and documents, making copies of all the necessary documents (make sure you retain the originals of all documents). You pay your application fee and wait for something to happen. After a period in which they have ignored you, you ask if you need to do anything else, and their answer is that the evaluation process is underway and can take anywhere from four to six weeks. The feeling of getting close to your license slowly fades away and you wonder what you will do for the two months the

USCG is evaluating your application. Should you go back to work as an AB? Should you get a part-time job to regain the money spent for school? Should you yell at the Coast Guard because their evaluation process sucks?

This is a real problem. As the information in your head is ready to pop out on the exam sheet, you fret as you need to keep it fresh for up to two more months. This is not a productive time for the applicant. I went into the USCG when I was getting close to completing everything and asked what the evaluation time was. The representative, knowing how bogged down the evaluators are, told me I would have to wait six to eight weeks.

Mariners face a real Catch-22. The ideal situation would be to submit your application with about four to six weeks of school left, so while the USCG is evaluating your application, you can take your final classes. When the evaluation is over, you could submit your final certificates on the spot and be ready to test that following day. The unfortunate reality is that mariners are not allowed to apply until all certificates are completed, meaning that they have to sit around for the evaluation, wasting their time, when they could be tested and out the door onto a mate's job. I have seen real situations in which mariners have been promised a third mate job upon completion after sailing as an AB for a company, only to find that the process of evaluation takes too long and the job was given to someone else, or the mariner had to take another AB job to fill the time. It is hard to wait at least two months before testing for your third mate's license.

I tried to explain this Catch-22 to the USCG. The USCG offered no solution. The officials stood there with perplexed looks. This is what I proposed to them: If a mariner is getting close to finishing the classes and assessments, they could apply with letters of confirmation that the student has paid and is enrolled in the final classes needed for completion of the STCW 95 for Officer in Charge of a Navigational Watch requirements at the school or schools. That way the evaluation process could get underway and the student is spending that time in class, finishing the program and studying for the exam. When the classes are finished, the student could then submit the final certificates upon request. The USCG officials mulled it over and responded, "Sure."

I went to the schools that were offering my last classes (two classes were left, at two different schools) and requested letters of confirmation. The schools mailed them to me and I submitted them with my application package to the REC. The USCG accepted the application and began the evaluation. When the evaluation was complete, the certificates that I needed were in my hand at the front desk. The USCG made copies and asked when I wanted to take the test. I said the following week.

That process cut two to three months off my wait time. The important point is to personally set this up with the USCG. As I discussed earlier, every REC is different. It worked in Seattle, but it is not policy! Explain the problem and offer the solution. Make sure you do this with enough time to get the evaluation over around the same time you complete the rest of your classes. This leaves little for the USCG to take issue with, and also lets the USCG know you are serious because you have already come this far. Ask what the approximate evaluation time is at the REC, and then coordinate your classes and study time to fill the gap.

Leave time for studying before you take the exam. I recommend no longer than two weeks. A human body works better with deadlines. However, do not push it out so far that you are beating a dead horse by exam time. There is such a thing as too much studying.

When it is time to study for the exam, you can do a number of things on your own. Some schools, like Crawford's Nautical in Seattle, let you study and use their resources to prep for the test after you have taken classes with them. Their instructors are on hand during class breaks to answer any questions you might have. Other schools could do the same, but check to make sure before walking in and studying.

I recommend purchasing a set of exam textbooks or testing software. One example is *The Deck Officer's Study Guide*, which are known to mariners as the Murphy books, by Captain Joseph F. Murphy, II. The Murphy books have all the USCG questions set up in a reader-friendly format and some background on each subject. Many mariners have passed their exams with the help of Captain Murphy's books, myself included. They are about $300 for the set and worth it. Murphy books are usually sold at all the maritime schools or nautical book stores around the country. But Murphy books are just one example of the textbooks available to mariners. You can pick up many sets of textbooks and software to help you study. More and more software and Internet-based study programs are out there, like Captain Joe's software at www. lapware.org or www.seasources.net, which is Web based. These programs are designed to work either as separate software or on the Internet. Captain Joe's LAPWARE is a great program that has all the test questions set up like a USCG exam, and includes illustrations. The great thing about this program is if you need help or have trouble with a certain problem or subject, the software explains every problem with all the applicable references. This is extremely helpful. LAPWARE can be ordered over the Internet or by contacting Blue Water Books in Ft. Lauderdale, Florida. Many maritime bookstores either offer or can obtain more software. Ask around. If you are looking for more of an Internet-based program, www.seasources.net is a free Web-based program. It has quizzes on all subjects, but no explanations so you need to know what you are doing. It is great for the multiple-choice USCG tests, and comes with all pertinent illustrations.

You also can ask about these when you are taking your courses, and a school official will direct you to them, or might have them, or similar programs at the training facility. You might run into used sets of books and software, which is fine, but be aware that there are updated questions to the exams from the USCG. Make sure you have the latest changes so you are studying the right material.

After taking all the classes, you should be well-versed in CFR and other published government regulations. My philosophy is know the answer or know where to find it. You can dump a lot of information out of your head and rely on these resource materials to get you through the tests. This book is not meant to be a study guide, but I will list each exam and talk about all the resources in the testing room available to you.

If you feel that you grasp the subjects well and are looking for just the exam questions, they are available for free on the USCG Web site. Go to the Merchant Mariner home page (http://www. uscg.mil/stcw/) and click on "Merchant Mariner Info Center." Click on "Deck Exam Info," and a list of books will appear for all subjects. You can download or print them in Microsoft Excel or Adobe PDF format. Either way, they are pretty big files and a lot of questions with no subject info at all, just the questions and answers. The site also has a section for the revised or new questions from the USCG. Print those out, even if you have the Murphy books or another study guide. Make sure you have all the questions either way.

Every person retains knowledge differently. Some are lucky and have photographic memories or better knowledge of the subject matter. Every person has to find what works best for them when studying. What worked for me was a schedule. The exam I took for third/second mate unlimited oceans detailed seven main topics. When mariners take the test, they have to obey the rules. Once you start your exam, you have to complete it. You cannot take two subjects one day and then schedule to take the next subjects in a week. Once it starts, you have to complete all the subjects in consecutive days.

You also have to take at least two subjects per day. The only one allowed to be taken alone is the last exam. You are allowed to take more than two per day, if you are confident enough to do it. A friend of mine walked in and took all the tests in one day for his 100 ton master inland license. He failed every one of them by one question. When I asked him why he did it, he said, "To see if I could."

I recommend taking no more than two per day over three full days, with the last test on the morning of the fourth. Then, when you pass your last exam, you can spend the afternoon of the fourth day getting your license. The exams are given in order, and there usually isn't any negotiating with the USCG examiner.

Talk to the examiner who runs the testing room when you make your appointment to test. Ask the order of the tests, ask if it is in writing, or write the schedule down.

If English is your second language, check with the REC to see if the oral examination is available.

I studied for two weeks solid, two subjects per day. I scoured the question bank, the Murphy books, and the problems until I was confident about passing the exams. The night before, I narrowed my focus to the first two exams, Rules of the Road (COL-REGS) and Deck General. I kept the progression going, getting done with those exams and studying the next two that night until I could drink no more coffee, and fit no more information into my head. It is not an easy process, but it is obtainable if you stick to a schedule. I have seen lots of competent mariners as boatswains or ABs not begin the upgrading process to their license because of fear and doubt. Do not fall into that category.

If you do not pass a particular exam, you are allowed to take each exam over two more times. Those exams can be scheduled and taken one each day. Some mariners fly through the whole test, fail half of the exams, and reschedule the tests on their own time, giving them a chance to study each test specifically. This is an option, but one I don't like. Failing a test is okay. Everyone has failed one test or another. It is all part of the scheme the Coast Guard has set up to ensure that you pass the exams and get your license. If you do not pass the exam after testing three times, you cannot retest until the ninety days have passed.

The reason I do not prefer this method is that some of the mates I have worked with definitely should not be mates. The testing structure allows for a mariner to take each exam three times before actually failing the exam. This provides ample space for the folks who really do not get the material to slide through on a prayer. It happens in every industry. There are always people who make you question how they got to where they are. This is no way to take up a profession. Instead, become a real mariner. Do the work, study until you know the material, ask questions, get tutoring if needed, use all resources available to you and you will be a licensed officer on the first round of exams, and a good one.

If you do end up failing one, don't fret. I recommend taking it again immediately. Do not let that information and your focus get lost by waiting. Get it over with.

The USCG has set it up so if you fail an exam three times, you have to pay another examination fee and can schedule another exam after a ninety-day-wait period. The evaluation is good for one year from the original approval date. If you get to the point where you are taking and retaking tests after many failures, do not become an officer. It is something that you are struggling too hard to accomplish. When you get your license, you are found qualified to do the job. If it takes a mariner that many times to pass, stop. Remember the surgeon example? Who do you want cutting out your spleen? The doctor that passed the exams the first time or the doctor that had to retake them several times before passing? Hmmm? I am not trying to discourage you, I want you to pass the test and get it over with!

Also, know the materials available to you in the testing room.

The applicable CFRs are:

33 CFR parts 1-124, 125-199

46 CFR parts 1-89, 90-189

49 CFR parts 100-185

Publications:

102 International Code of Signals

Light List Vol. 5

Coast Pilot Vol. 1,4,6,7

Radio Navigation Aids Pub. 117

Publication 229, Sight reductions

Nautical Almanac

Chemical Data Guide

Stability Reference Guide

Nautical Training charts

Great Circle weather tracking charts

Maneuvering boards

Universal plotting sheets

Illustation manuals

Ask your instructors about each of these books for more detail. Know these books and what they offer you for information. They will be lifesavers in the testing room.

This list represents the main reference material available during the test. I know there are some specialized material for other exams, such as engineering, Mobile Offshore Drilling Units (MODU), rivers and pilots. If you are testing for any of these or need a better detailed list, contact the REC and ask to speak with the examiner. I have not found the list of books in the test room on the Web site yet, but the examiner has the list and can help you in more detail.

For the unlimited, near coastal, and oceans mate's licenses, the exams will be held at the REC. For some of the limited tonnage inland licenses and certifications like Life Boatman, the exams can be done right at the maritime schools. They are called category one (I) classes. Any class that is a category one class means that the Coast Guard has approved the school to do the examination on site and will honor the certificate when brought to the Coast Guard. If you are testing for a limited tonnage, inland license, find out if it is a category one exam. It is information worth knowing so you do not have to go to the USCG to take the test if you do not need to. Also, some of the approved hawsepiping programs, such as the Simulation, Training, Assessment and Research (STAR) Center in Toledo, Ohio or the Maritime Institute of Technology and Graduates Studies (MITAGS) in Baltimore, Maryland, will have the Coast Guard examiner come to the school and proctor the exam at the campus. A nice benefit if you are in one of those programs.

Chapter Nine
Transferring from the Military to the Merchant Marines

I started my career in the Coast Guard. I feel lucky because I had such great teachers and training onboard my first vessel. After ten years I still have never seen a ship run better than the USCGC *Mallow* (WLB-396), aka The Black Pig of Death. My superiors loved their jobs and could train like the most seasoned instructors. For the most part, the transfer to the merchant marines from the military has its ups and downs.

Obviously, the best branches are the Navy and Coast Guard to transfer with sea time and training. To be one of those individuals, you have to have been on a ship in a bridge-related job to get credit for the sea time.

Because a military person might be attached to a vessel for two to three years straight that could equal a lot of sea time. The problem is, those ships are not out at sea the whole time, but the military looks at it as straight sea time. The USCG looks at it differently.

Because the ship is not out at sea the entire time a person is attached to the vessel, the USCG came up with a general scheme for military sea time. Turn to the end of this chapter for an excerpt of the *USCG's Marine Safety Manual, Volume Three,* chapter two, reprinted here for your convenience.

The important thing to know about transferring is to get as much paperwork and certification out of the way as you can before you leave the military. For example, in the military an individual is subject to random drug screenings at any time. That is a good thing because you can get a drug letter from your command stating verbatim what the Coast Guard wants to hear from chapter five. It will satisfy the drug test for the USCG for an MMD or license.

While in the military, take as much training as possible. When a unit offers a training class, take it. Cross reference it with classes that you need to complete an MMD or license. If in doubt, call the REC. Those classes will cut down on the amount of work needed after discharge from the military. The proof of sea time is important also. Get the required forms you need before you get out.

When I got out of the Coast Guard and was applying for my license, I brought my military discharge form DD214 over to the Seattle REC to use for proof of sea time. The guy behind the counter said, "We don't take these as proof of sea time."

I was shocked. I thought there wasn't a more solid document than a DD214. That says exactly which ships you were on, the exact dates, and what rate you were. Basically everything that proves you were at sea.

"What do you accept as proof of sea time?" I asked.

"A letter on Coast Guard letterhead from your command stating that you were attached to those vessels," the guy behind the counter said.

"So, you would like an additional letter saying the exact same thing that the DD214 says," I replied.

"Yes."

I did not know how to read this except to guess that the USCG obviously had a problem with DD214s and needed another form of proof. I went to my command in Seattle, and they drafted me a letter with all the goodies the REC wanted. I brought it back and submitted it. The USCG was satisfied, but I was still a bit confused. Years later, I was applying for my upgrade and another fellow was there applying for a MMD. He was saying something about his sea time. I, being the sticky beak that I am, spoke up and asked him if he had a separate letter proving his military time because the USCG does not accept DD214s. The new guy at the counter looked at me and said, "Yes we do."

I said, "Not when I was applying."

He said, "I know, years ago we didn't accept them, but now we do."

I shrugged my shoulders again and said, "Okay."

The reality is, the USCG did not like the form DD214 because it did not give enough detail regarding sea time. The REC has a request form you have to fill out to get your proof of service.

This request for proof of service is mailed to the military archives, and they will send you your proof of service documents that the Coast Guard accepts as sea time.

This is just one example of how confusing it can get when navigating the bureaucracy of the Coast Guard. You have got to have the right documents before you get out or your ship might sail. A couple of short cuts with military sea service: If you are still active and plan to go to the merchants or anything like it, request a letter of sea service from your commanding officer with the specifics of the vessel, your duties and responsibilities, dates and all that (refer to "letters of sea time"). Make sure it is on ship's letterhead and has all the appropriate stamps (that makes it look more official). I talked with a rep from the REC, and he said they would accept a letter like that, just like any official letter of sea service.

As you will see in the Marine Safety Manual at the end of this chapter, all military sea time is reduced by 60 percent, which means a person transferring from the military only get 60 percent of the total sea time acquired. For example, when I got out of the Coast Guard, I had four years of sea service, which totaled 1,440 days. When I applied for my license, the REC said I could only use 60 percent of it, which was 864 days. Be aware of this and acquire your sea time accordingly. If a veteran wanted to obtain an unlimited third mate license, they would need 1,080 days on vessels with appropriate tonnage. Doing the math ahead of time, the veteran would need 1800 days (1,800 x 0.6 = 1,080) active military sea service.

Be aware that some rates (jobs) in the service do not qualify for sea service or partial sea service. The job must be related to shipboard, especially bridge and deck duties. Refer to the *Marine Safety Manual* for each job and branch and what it qualifies for. That is the fastest way to represent your sea time in the military.

If you are already out, getting out, or just did not get all the information before you were discharged, another quick way is to go online to the Department of Veterans Affairs (VA) and request a copy of your military record. I spoke with a VA representative and she told me that is does not matter if you are active, reservist, or a veteran, all requests for proof of service go through the VA. Unless you have some pull at your command or know someone in archives this seems to be the route to take. They have created an online form, which makes it go a little faster. Go to www.archives. gov/research_room/vetrecs/ and follow the instructions. Have the dates you enlisted and got out handy, along with all the personal info. The Web site will send an electronic request and mail you your forms, which you can bring down to the Coast Guard as proof of sea service. Try to have the request sent to the National Personnel Records Center in St. Louis, Missouri, on Page St. The woman I spoke to at the VA told me that it takes less time.

If you do not have a computer, all these forms are in hard copy from the VA or the REC. It just takes longer to receive and submit them that way. If you do not have a computer of your own, you can go to the public library or an Internet café. Doing things electronically can save a lot of time.

This is very important: before you get out of the military, have these documents:

Sea service letters from all vessels.

- Letters of watchstanding from all vessels (chapter five).
- Physical examination on the merchant marine physical form CG719K. If in doubt, get the form from the Internet or REC and bring it with you for your final physical before you get out. It will be good for one year after that (chapter five).
- Drug test letter from your command (chapter five).
- All your training certificates in original.
- All your PQS and official letters.

This will save you so much time in transferring from the military to the merchants. You can start doing this stuff before you get out and be ready to apply and test right away. The big bonus is, if you have spent a significant part of your life in the military, you can transfer to an organization like MSC, which is a civilian merchant fleet, and your government pension will continue. You can combine your military service and your merchant marine time towards your government retirement. Ask before you sign on with a MSC vessel. Some of the union MSC vessels do not allow you to do this. It has to be with MSC itself.

As you transfer from the military to civilian life, the military tries to equip you with whatever they can to help you advance your career. Some career "advisors" might guide you in a field or profession you want to pursue given your experience in the military. In my experience, these folks know little or nothing about the merchant marines. Take what you can and ask them as many questions as you wish. You can obtain merchant mariners document many ways, and as a veteran, financial aid is available to you. The GI Bill can be used for training at any maritime training school and academy. If you go to a school that has financial aid, since you are a veteran, you can qualify for additional grants based on your independent financial situation, such as the Pell grant, state grants, and military scholarships. Talk to the schools, the VA, advisors, WorkSource (mentioned in chapter seven). Talk to anybody who could help you. As a veteran, I would hate to have mariners pay for training they could get for free. Use all your resources. Stay ahead of the game.

CHAPTER 2: EQUIVALENT SERVICE FOR LICENSES/MERCHANT MARINER'S

DOCUMENTS

LIST OF FIGURES

MARINE SAFETY MANUAL
CHAPTER 2: EQUIVALENT SERVICE FOR LICENSES/MERCHANT

MARINER'S DOCUMENTS

A. Military Service.

Sea service requirements for original licenses and raises of grade are stated in 46 CFR Part 10, and are based on service aboard U.S. merchant vessels. 46 CFR Part 12 gives the requirements for unlicensed ratings. Military sea service experience must be a reasonable equivalent to the service required of a merchant mariner who is seeking an identical license or MMD. Military personnel applying for a license or MMD represent a challenge to the REC evaluating their application. This is due to the wide range of ratings and duties they present as sea service. The evaluations are normally conducted by the REC. The REC may refer the more difficult or sensitive evaluations to NMC. In addition, to avoid the appearance of favoritism or undue influence, the REC should refer an evaluation to NMC for any applicant that is:

1. A Coast Guard officer senior to the OCMI;
2. A Coast Guard officer stationed at the MSO or Activity senior to the chief of the REC; or
3. A person assigned to work at the REC.

B. Criteria For Accepting Military Sea Experience.

1. Application Evaluation.

   Evaluations of military experience are conducted when a Transcript Of Sea Service or equivalent information is presented with an application (see Section B.2). At the discretion of the REC, additional information may be requested. Generally, additional information will be required to verify claims of a higher percentage of underway time than the 60% normally allowed by the regulations. In addition, the REC may require an official description of duties statement, letters of qualification, service record entries, or letters from former supervisors or commanding officers.

2. Transcript Of Sea Service.

   The Transcript Of Sea Service provides the periods of assignment, name of vessel, and capacity (rate/rank) served. The application must contain a Transcript Of Sea Service, not a shipboard generated letter or DD-214. Standard Form SF-180, Request Pertaining To Military Records, may be used by the applicant to obtain a transcript. This form lists

the addresses of all the services where the request should be sent. The Federal Record Center, at St. Louis, MO, is not sending the ex-service person Transcripts of Sea Service. Instead, they are sending various pages from their personnel files which document when, where, rate, and duration of the applicant's sea service. Evaluators will

have to become familiar with the various forms and how to extract the pertinent information. Because these forms are military in nature, MSO administration offices or

PERSRUs could be of assistance in deciphering the information. The SIP may accept other documentation attesting to sea service if it has the same level of authenticity as a transcript. In other words, will it stand up to an audit?

2-2

3. Tonnage.

The majority of military vessels are not measured in gross or net tonnage. Therefore, it is necessary for the evaluating officer to estimate the gross tonnage of the vessels for

which experience is claimed. The formula "DISPLAC-MENT x .57" provides an acceptable estimate of gross tonnage (use full load displacement). Jane's Fighting Ships

is an excellent reference for finding the vital statistics of U.S. military vessels. It is likely that this source will provide the displacement for most military vessels. All Coast Guard

high endurance cutters (WHECs), medium endurance cutters (WMECs) of the Bear class only (270 foot cutter), icebreakers (WAGBs), and the USCGC Eagle are over 1600

gross tons. All other Coast Guard vessels currently in service are less than 1600 gross tons. Former Coast Guard vessels of 255 feet (77 meters) and up were over 1600 gross

tons.

4. Calculation of Service.

Military sea service shall be evaluated sequentially in the order obtained over the course

of a military career, which reflects the same progression for a merchant mariner. Tonnage and horsepower limitations, if any, shall be calculated for each license level through the progression. It is not acceptable to average tonnage or horsepower over a career. Pay particular attention to the recency requirements in 46 CFR 10.202(e) because recency, or lack thereof, can also limit the tonnage or horsepower for an original license.

5. Description Of Duties Evaluation.

The most troublesome aspect of the military evaluation is translating military duties to meet the experience requirements specified in 46 CFR Part 10. Based upon past evaluations, the following guidelines have been developed. See Figure 2-2 and 2-3 of this chapter for further explanations and examples.

a. Officers. Deck watch officers' (DWOs) and engineering watch officers' (EWOs) duties are considered equivalent to the watchstanding duties performed by licensed mates and engineers respectively aboard merchant vessels. Therefore, this qualifying sea service may be used to satisfy the experience requirements for an original or raise of grade of a mate or assistant engineer license. For an original third's license, up to eighteen months service as DWO/EWO may be substituted for up to 36 months of unlicensed service. One day of service as a DWO or EWO is counted as 2 days of unlicensed sea service to meet the requirements of the regulations. When computing sea service toward a license grade above third, such as an original second, or a raise of grade, DWO/EWO time is creditable on a one-for-one basis. Service experience obtained as a junior officer of the deck (JOOD) is considered equivalent (on a one-for- one basis) to able seaman time. See examples at the end of this chapter.

2-3

b. Service As Commanding Officer (CO). To qualify as unlimited master, at least six months of the required creditable service must have been as CO. The CO service must have occurred after the applicant had accumulated enough creditable service to qualify as chief mate. An applicant with military experience has not had exposure to merchant marine concerns such as cargo handling, payrolls, union relations, etc. Service as CO indicates that the applicant has experience in a position of responsibility which compensates, to some extent, for differences between the operation of military and merchant vessels.

c. Service As Engineer Officer (EO). To qualify as unlimited chief engineer, at least six months of the required creditable service must have been as EO. The EO service must have occurred after the applicant had accumulated enough creditable service to qualify as first assistant engineer. An applicant with military experience has not had exposure to merchant marine concerns such as payrolls, union relations, etc. Service as EO indicates that the applicant has experience in a position of responsibility which compensates, to some extent, for differences between the operation of military and merchant vessels.

d. Enlisted Personnel Applying For Licenses. Evaluation of sea service is more complex for enlisted personnel than it is for officers. This is due to the great variety of specialized duties that enlisted personnel perform. When evaluating underway sea service, use the following guidelines:

i. Service as a seaman apprentice (SA) or seaman (SN) is equivalent to sea service as an ordinary seaman or deckhand;

ii. Service as fireman apprentice (FA) or fireman (FN) is equivalent to sea service as a wiper or coal passer;

iii. Service as a petty officer in the deck department is considered equivalent to that of an AB; and

iv. Service as a petty officer in the engineering department is considered equivalent to that of a QMED.

v. Deck rating of E-4 and above with qualifications as DWO is equivalent to licensed mate time.

vi. Service experience obtained as a junior officer of the deck (JOOD) is considered

vii. equivalent (on a one-for-one basis) to able seaman time.

viii. Engine rating of E-4 and above with qualifications as EWO is equivalent to licensed assistant engineer time.

Note: The above are only guidelines. Applicants furnishing time as a petty officer in charge of a navigational watch should have that time counted towards a licensed officer.

2-4

e. Ratings Accepted Toward Licenses. Certain ratings due to their nature are usually disqualifying on their face for a license. Figure 2-1 is a guide for evaluating service in various ratings. Suggested acceptance of service is indicated by "XXX." When evaluating military ratings, if the military service is found to be closely related to the duties of AB or QMED, then RECs are authorized to grant up to 50% of the service towards the applicable license.

2-5

FIGURE 2-1: SUGGESTED ACCEPTANCE OF MILITARY SEA SERVICE BY RATING FOR LICENSE QUALIFICATIONS NAVY AND COAST GUARD RATINGS And THEIR EQUIVALENCIES

DECK
100%
DECK
50%
QMED
100%
QMED1 PURSER
100%
PURSER2 PURSER
50%
Jr. Asst.
PURSER
Aerographer's Mate (AG)
Air Traffic Controller (AC)
Aircraft Survival Equipmentman (PR)
Aviation Antisubmarine Warfare Operator (AW)
Aviation Antisubmarine Warfare Technician (AX)
Aviation Boastswain's Mate (AB), (ABE), (ABF), (ABH)
Aviation Electrician's Mate (AE)
Aviation Electronics Technician (AT)
Aviation Fire Control Tech. (AQ)
Aviation Machinist's Mate (AD)
Aviation Maintenance Admin. (AZ)
Aviation Ordnanceman (AO)
Aviation Storekeeper (AK)

Aviation Structural Mechanic (AM), (AME), (AMH), (AMS)
Aviation Support Equipment Tech. (AS)
Aviation Survivalman (ASM) (CG)
Boatswain's Mate (BM) XXX
Boiler Technician (BT) XXX
Builder (BU)
Construction Electrician (CE)
Construction Mechanic (CM)
Cryptologic Technician (CT), (CTA), (CTR), (CT), (CTI), (CTM), (CTT)
Damage Controlman (DC) XXX
Data Processing Technician (DP) XXX
Data Systems Technician (DS)
Dental Technician (DT)
Disbursing Clerk (DK) XXX
Electrician's Mate (EM) -CG XXX
Electrician's Mate (EM) -Navy XXX
Electronics Technician (ET)

2-6

FIGURE 2-1: SUGGESTED ACCEPTANCE OF MILITARY SEA SERVICE BY RATING FOR LICENSE QUALIFICATIONS NAVY AND COAST GUARD RATINGS And THEIR EQUIVALENCIES

DECK
100%
DECK
50%
QMED
100%
QMED1 PURSER
100%
PURSER2 PURSER
50%
Jr. Asst.
PURSER
Electronic Warfare Technician (EW)
Engineering Aid (EA)
Engineman (EN) XXX
Equipment Operator (EO)
Fire Controlman (FC)

Fire Control Tech. (FT) (FTH), (FTG)
Fire And Safety Technician (FS)
Gas Turbine Systems Tech. (GS), (GSE), (GSM) XXX
Gunner's Mate (GM) XXX
Health Services Technician (HS) XXX5
Hospital Corpsman (HM) XXX5
Hull Maintenance Technician (HT) XXX
Illustrator Draftsman (DM)
Instrument Man (IM)
Intelligence Specialist (IS)
Interior Comm. Electrician (IC) XXX
Investigator (IV)
Journalist (JO)
Legalman (LN)
Lithographer (LI)
Machinery Technician (MK) XXX
Machinery Repairmen (MR) XXX
Machinist's Mate (MM)
Marine Science Technician (MST)
Master-At-Arms (MA)
Mess Management Specialist (MS) XXX
Mineman (MN)
Missile Technician (MT)
Molder (Ml)
Musician (MU)
Navy Counselor (CC)
Ocean Systems Technician (OT)
Operations Specialist (OS) XXX
Opticalman (OM)

2-7

FIGURE 2-1: SUGGESTED ACCEPTANCE OF MILITARY SEA SERVICE BY RATING FOR LICENSE QUALIFICATIONS NAVY AND COAST GUARD RATINGS AND THEIR EQUIVALENCIES
DECK
100%
DECK
50%
QMED
100%

QMED1 PURSER
100%
PURSER2 PURSER
50%
Jr. Asst.
PURSER
Patternmaker (PM)
Personnelman (PN)
Photographer's Mate (Ph)
Port Securityman (PS)
Postal Clerk (PDT)
Public Affairs Specialist (PA)
Quartermaster (QM) XXX
Radarman (RD) XXX
Radioman (Rm) (USCG ServiceSee TC)
Religious Program Specialist (RP)
Ship's Serviceman (SH) XXX
Signalman (SM) XXX
Sonar Technician (ST), (STS)
Steelworker (SW)
Storekeeper (SK) XXX
Subsistence Specialist (SS) XXX
Telecommunications Specialist (TC)
Telephone Technician (TT) XXX
Torpedoman's Mate (TM)
Utilitiesman (UT)
Weapons Technician (WT)
Yeoman (YN)

1ST RULE: CALCULATE 60% OF QUALIFYING TIME THEN
APPLY ADDITIONAL % AS SHOWN ABOVE
1. QMED 100% Only For Standing Engine room Watches; Watchstanding Must Be Documented.
2. PURSER 100%; Must Be A PO1 Through MCPO, Or, PO2 For 5
   Years In Supervising On Ordering.
3. QMED 100% Only For Standing Engine room Watches; Watchstanding Must Be Documented.
4. PURSER 100%; Must Be A PO1 Through MCPO, Or, PO2 For 5
   Years In Supervising And Ordering.
5. HS and HM Rates, 1st Class Or Higher, Qualify For Hospital
   Corpsman Endorsement With At Least 1 Month Service In Mili-

tary Hospital Or U.S. Public Health Services Hospital (Time At Sea Not Required); Must Be Issued Jr. Asst. Purser For This Endorsement.

6. QMED 100% Only For Standing Engine room Watches; Watchstanding Must Be Documented.

7. PURSER 100%; Must Be A Po1 Through MCPO, Or, PO2For 5 Years In Supervising And Ordering.

2-8

    f. Ratings Accepted Toward MMDs.

        i.   Deck Service. Enlisted service, regardless of rating, must meet the definition in 46 U.S.C. 7301 of "service on deck" in order for it to be accepted toward any of the able seaman classifications.

        ii.   Engineer Service. Any enlisted service which can be equated to wiper or to any of the qualified member of the engine department (QMED) ratings may be accepted toward meeting the service requirements for all the QMED endorsements except deck engine mechanic and engineman. Qualifications for deck engine mechanic and engineman must be evaluated separately since these two ratings have specific qualification requirements which must be met.

    g. Submarine Service.

        i.   (1) Enlisted Service. Care should be taken when applying Figure 2-1 to submarine service. Often on submarines non-traditional ratings such as YNs or SKs stand operational watches. Watchstanding qualifications and interviewing the applicant should help the evaluator determine what is acceptable submarine service.

        ii.   Deck Service. Only 75 percent of the total creditable sea service required for a deck license may be obtained aboard submarines. The remaining creditable sea service must have been obtained aboard surface vessels.

        iii.   Example. An applicant for an unlimited third mate license has a total of 20 months of creditable sea service on board submarines as DWO. The applicant is required to present 18 months of creditable sea service as DWO. Only 75% may be on submarines, therefore, only 13.5 months (18 months x .75) can be used toward the third's license. The additional 4.5 months must be obtained as a DWO on surface vessels.

iv. Engineering Service. In contrast, underway engineering service aboard submarines is considered equivalent to engineering service obtained aboard surface vessels.

v. See 46 CFR 10.213(d) for further information.

h. Service On Vessels Other Than Underway. 46 CFR 10.213(c) discusses the application of a 25% credit factor for periods of assignment to vessels at times other than underway. Creditable sea service for this category applies to vessels, whose sea service has not been previously used, that spend the vast majority of their time moored. An example, would be a submarine tender or a vessel undergoing an extended shipyard visit. The vessel status would not be reflected on the Record of Sea Service but might be established during the evaluator's interview of the applicant.

2-9

i. Credit For Military Schools. Unless the school is NMC approved, training received at a military school will not be granted sea service credit nor be accepted as meeting mandatory training requirements (e.g. radar observer, firefighting).

C. Experience Aboard Dredges.

Self propelled dredges may conduct their operations upon inland waters. Service on board dredges should be evaluated to ensure appropriate ocean or near coastal service. Daily operations that include at least one voyage beyond the boundary lines for the disposal or mining of dredge material shall be credited as ocean service.

D. Evaluating Coast Guard Personnel For Licenses. Coast Guard personnel who apply for a license shall comply with all the regulations for the license. Officers senior to the OCMI, shall request permission from the district commander to apply for a license. In granting such requests, the district commander may require the applicant to comply with certain additional conditions. Some of these conditions may include submitting applications and taking examinations at a Regional Examination Center (REC) in another district.

E. Examining Coast Guard Marine Safety Personnel For Licenses Coast Guard marine safety experience does not equate to shipboard service and may not be used to qualify for an original or raise of grade of a license. Such experience is generally helpful in preparing for a license examination; however, the only military service creditable towards eligibility for a license is underway service (except as discussed in paragraph 2.B.4.h. above). To prevent criticism or charges of Coast Guard favoritism in the licensing process, Coast Guard marine safety personnel must obtain permission to apply for a license from their district commander. The district commander may apply the restrictions listed above. However, under the present examination system, a separate randomly produced examination can allow the applicant to sit at the local REC. The applicant's file shall contain the letter of request and the district commander's letter of approval. Headquarters personnel should apply to the district commander in whose jurisdiction the REC resides. Refer to paragraph A.2. of this chapter for instances when applications must be sent to Commandant to be evaluated. Coast Guard personnel who have passed a rules of the road test as an end of course test or as a Deck Watch Officer examination will not be exempted from taking the rules of the road portion of any Coast Guard license examination.

F. Examining Coast Guard Regional Examination Center Personnel For Licenses. Special examinations should be requested from the examinations branch at the National Maritime Center for REC personnel. See chapter 5 for further details.

G. Time-And-One-Half Sea Service Credit.

The time-and-one-half provision was put in the regulations to take into account the additional experience mariners obtain when they stand watches on a six-on, six-off watch schedule. Time-and-one-half credit will not be given for overtime or for other work days that do not involve six-on, six-off watchstanding even if the work days are more than eight hours long. The six-on, six-off watch schedule should be proven to the satisfaction of the OCMI or their representative before the time and a half credit is applied. The following sources express this intent.

2-10

1. The Notice of Proposed Rulemaking (for the current licensing system), FR 35926, August 8, 1983, stated, "Many comments expressed concern about obtaining additional credit for 12 hour days in the case of people that work six on/six off watches. A statement has been added to a new definition section in the proposed regulations whereby any persons standing watches on any vessels upon which the six on/six off watch schedule may be used, will be given credit for 1.5 times each 12 hour day of service in that capacity."

2. House Report No. 96-1075 on Public Law 96-378 [H.R. 5164], which created our current system of Able Seaman ratings, states on page 27, "The eight-hour provision is primarily intended to assure that those mariners who work a two-watch system (that is, six hours on duty and six hours off duty for a total of twelve hours a day) will receive a day and a half of credit for each twelve-hour day worked."

3. Some inland vessels not subject to the 2 or 3 watch system have in place a 12 hour watch rotation. If the REC can verify that such a schedule is practiced and legal, day and a half credit may be granted.

2-11

FIGURE 2-2: EXAMPLES OF MILITARY EVALUATIONS (DECK)

Note: The service presented must be equivalent to that required of a merchant mariner. The following methods of evaluation apply. All the sea service times referred to below are after all the appropriate deductions have been made.

Original Third Mate (except academy graduates)

Officer Sea Service:

Each day of DWO sea service is counted as two days of the required service for an original third mate's license. As an example 18 months sea service as DWO is equal to the 36 months of unlicensed sea service. Service as DWO is equivalent to licensed merchant marine watchstanding service rather than unlicensed service, therefore, more sea service credit can be given.

Officer sea service as other than a DWO is counted day-for-day towards an original third mate's license. The following are some examples of this type of deck service: CIC Officer, Navigator, JOOD, Assistant Navigator, 1st Lieutenant, Gunnery Officer and other duties associated with the operation of the vessel on deck.

This time cannot be used to duplicate service during the same time period that is being counted as watchstanding. When the non-watchstanding time exceeds that of the watchstanding time, the difference in the times may be used as 1 for 1 service. For example, if the Transcript of Sea Service shows 20 months as operations officer and 16 months as DWO during the same time period, the difference of four months can be credited, after applying a 60% reduction, on a 1 for 1 basis.

Enlisted Sea Service:

Most of the ratings are explained in 46 CFR 10.213(b). The Navy has combined some ratings into operations specialist. Operations specialist is a combination of the ratings quartermaster, radarman, sonarman, and signalman. The evaluator must be careful when evaluating the operations specialist to ascertain the type of duties the applicant performed as it relates to the navigation and control of the vessel.

Combining Sea Service:

When computing the 36 months (1080 days) required for a third's license, you may use a variety of service in combination. Care must be taken not to allow excess service when computing the license. Service is computed in the chronological order in which it was served. The following is an example:

2-12

FIGURE 2-2: EXAMPLES OF MILITARY EVALUATIONS (Cont'd) (DECK EXAMPLE OF THIRD MATE CALCULATIONS (NON-ACADEMY) TRANSCRIPT OF MILITARY SEA SERVICE
NAME: CDR Joe Goodship
CGC GALLATIN (WHEC) SA/SN 8 MONTHS
GM3 24 MONTHS
CGC POINT HURON (WPB) GM3/2 24 MONTHS
CGC TACKLE (WYTL) GM2/1 28 MONTHS
CGC POLAR STAR (WAGB) ENS/LTJG 15 MONTHS

10 MONTHS DWO (UNDERWAY)

12 MONTHS 1ST LT.

3 MONTHS OPS OFFICER

CGC SASSAFRAS (WLB) LT 12 MONTHS

12 MONTHS OPS OFFICER

8 MONTHS DWO

The following is an example of how to compute the sea service time for the above transcript:

COMPUTATION OF SEA SERVICE

SEA SERVICE REDUCED BY 60% (DAYS) = TOTAL SEA SERVICE (MONTHS)

X .6(60%) X 30 DAYS

SEA

TOTAL SERVICE SEA

SEA REDUCED SERVICE

SERVICE BY 60% ALLOWED

RANK/RATE (MONTHS) (DAYS) (DAYS)

(1) CGC GALLATIN SA/SN 8 144 144 1

(over 1600 GT) GM3 24 432 1802+126 3

2-13

FIGURE 2-2: EXAMPLES OF MILITARY EVALUATIONS (DECK) (Cont'd)

1. 46 CFR 10.213(b) allows SA/SN sea service as equivalent to ordinary seaman service.

2. Section 2.B.4.d. allows up to 180 days of non-deck rating time (as defined in 46 CFR 10.213(b)) toward a Third Mate license.

3. The remainder of the 432 days after the 180 days is allowed can be given 50% credit as indicated in Figure 2-1 (432 - 180 = 252. 252 x 50% = 126). [NOTE: Had the GM3 service been a deck rating, such as BM3, the sea service would be equivalent to the able seaman sea service required by 46 CFR 10.407(a)(1).]

    ii.   CGC POINT HURON GM3/2 24 432 0

    iii. CGC TACKLE GM2/1 28 504 0 Both vessels are under 200 gross tons therefore the sea service cannot be used for this license.

    iv. CGC POLAR STAR DWO 10 180 360 (over 1600 GT) 1ST LT 5 90 90 Since the time here was as a DWO, each day of DWO sea service is counted as two days of required service or double the accrued time.

As stated previously, this sea service is considered equivalent to watchstanding mate service.

i.   CGC SASSAFRAS DWO 8 144 288 (over 200 GT) OPS OFFICER 4 72 72 TOTAL 1260 The Sassafras is under 1600 but it is over 200 gross tons so it can be used for up to 50% of the service required for an unlimited third's license. If more than 50% of the required service was on vessels under 1600 gross tons, a tonnage limitation would be computed for the third's license.

2-14

FIGURE 2-2: EXAMPLES OF MILITARY EVALUATIONS (DECK) (Cont'd) EXAMPLE OF ORIGINAL MASTER CALCULATIONS (ACADEMY) RANSCRIPT OF MILITARY SEA SERVICE NAME: CDR B. JONES

Summary of service:

Vessels Service Days Assigned Credit

Graduated CG Academy: Cadet

('77)Northwind (WAGB) >1600 DWO 700 420

('78)Burton Is. (WAGB) >1600 DWO 369 221

('84)Laurel (WLB) <1600 DWO 723 434

('91)Sedge (WLB) <1600 DWO 1067

640

('97)Acushnet (WMEC) <1600 CO 822 493

Sequential evaluation

For 3rd Mate

Vessels Credit Notes

CG Academy

Northwind: Qualified DWO

Qualifies as third mate: 46 CFR 10.407(a)(1)(iii)

For 2nd Mate

Vessels Credit Notes

Northwind 360

Total: 360 days/360 >1600

For Chief Mate

Vessels Credit Notes

Northwind 60 Carry over

Burton Is. 221

Laurel 79

Total: 360 Days/281 >1600

CDR Jones meets the sea service for chief mate AGTs. However, he has not served aboard a vessel of over 1600 gross tons since Burton Island in 1978. The recency provisions of 46

2-15

CFR 10.202(e) apply. He must have three months' qualifying experience on vessels of appropriate tonnage (all over 200grt, half over 1600grt) within three years of application.

2-16

FIGURE 2-2: EXAMPLES OF MILITARY EVALUATIONS (DECK) (Cont'd) For Master Vessels Credit Notes

Laurel 355

Sedge 640

Acushnet 493 CO

Total: 1488 <1600

CDR Jones qualifies for Master 1600 gross tons because he does not have sufficient service on vessels of over 1600 gross tons. However, he may be permitted to sit for Master Unlimited with a 2,000 gross register ton restriction as permitted by 46 CFR 10.402(b).
1. Mariner qualifies for third mate after completing the Coast

Guard academy and qualifying as a deck watch officer un

2. Service is evaluated sequentially, in the order obtained over the course of the career. In this case, the mariner "uses up" service on vessels of over 1600 gross tons early in the career. In effect, the higher tonnage service was used to qualify at second and chief mate levels.

3. To qualify for an original master's license, the mariner must serve as Commanding Officer for at least 180 days, 46 CFR 10.213(a).

2-17

FIGURE 2-3 EXAMPLES OF MILITARY EVALUATIONS (ENGINE)

Note: The service presented must be equivalent to that required of a merchant mariner. The following methods of evaluation apply. All the sea service times referred to below are after all the appropriate deductions have been made.

Original Third Assistant Engineer (except academy graduates)

Officer Sea Service:

Each day of EWO sea service is counted as two days of the required service for an original Third Assistant Engineer's licenses. As an example, 18 months sea service as

EWO is equal to the 36 months creditable sea service. Service as EWO is equivalent to licensed merchant marine watchstanding service rather than unlicensed service, therefore, more sea service credit can be given. Officer sea service as other than a EWO is counted day for day towards an original third's license. The following are some examples of this type of engineering service: Main Propulsion Assistant, Electrical Officer, Auxiliary Officer, Damage Control Officer and any other duties associated with the engineering plant.

This time cannot be used to duplicate service during the same time period that is being counted as watchstanding. When the non-watchstanding time exceeds that of the watchstanding time, the difference in the times may be used as 1 for 1 service. For example, if the Transcript of Sea Service shows 20 months as main propulsion assistant and 16 months as EWO during the same time period, the difference of four months can be credited, after applying the 60% reduction, on a one for one basis.

Enlisted Sea Service:

Most of the ratings are explained in 46 CFR 10.213(b). The Coast Guard has the rating

of Machinery Technician (MK) that combines the Boiler Technicians (BT), Machinist

Mate (MM), Damage Controlman (DC) and Engineman (EN).

Combining Sea Service:

When computing the 36 months (1080 days) required for a third's license, a variety of service may be used in combination. Care must be taken not to allow excess service when computing the license. Service is computed in the chronological order in which it was served. The following is an example:

2-18

FIGURE 2-3: EXAMPLES OF MILITARY EVALUATIONS (ENGINE) (Cont'd) EXAMPLES OF THIRD ASSISTANT ENGINEERS (NON-ACADEMYTRANSCRIPT OF MILITARY SEA SERVICE NAME: CDR Joe Goodship

CGC GALLATIN (WHEC) FA/FN 8 MONTHS

DC3 24 MONTHS

CGC POLAR STAR (WAGB) CWO2(ENG) 15 MONTHS

10 MONTHS EWO (UNDERWAY)

12 MONTHS

MAIN PROPULSION ASST.

3 MONTHS

AUXILIARY OFFICER

CGC TAMAROA (WMEC) CWO2(ENG) 12 MONTHS

12 MONTHS AUX OFFICER

8 MONTHS EWO (UNDERWAY)

The following is an example of how to compute the sea service time for the above transcript.

COMPUTATION OF SEA SERVICE

SEA SERVICE REDUCED BY 60% (DAYS) = TOTAL SEA SERVICE (MONTHS)

x .6(60%) x 30 DAYS

SEA

TOTAL SERVICE SEA

SEA REDUCED SERVICE

SERVICE BY 60% ALLOWED

RANK/RATE (MONTHS) (DAYS) (DAYS)

CGC GALLATIN FA/FN 8 144 1441

7000 hp (5300 kW) DC3 24 432 1802
1. 46 CFR 10.213(b) allows FA/FN sea service as equivalent to ordinary seaman service.
2. Section 2.B.4.d. allows up to 180 days of non-engine room rating time (as defined in 46CFR 10.213(b)) toward a Third Assistant Engineer's license. The computation gives 432 days but only 180 days can be used. [NOTE: In this example DC3 Goodship was not an engine room watchstander so per Figure 2-1, the service is not credited as engineer service. Had the DC3 service been as a watchstander or had it been an engine room rating such as MM3, the sea service would be equivalent to the QMED sea service required by 46 CFR 10.516(a)(1).]

2-19

FIGURE 2-3: EXAMPLES OF MILITARY EVALUATIONS (ENGINE) (Cont'd)

CGC POLAR STAR EWO 10 180 360

18,000 hp Dept. Head 5 90 90

(13,500 kW)

Since the time here was as an EWO, each day of EWO sea service is credited as two days of required service or double the accrued time. As stated previously, this sea service is considered equivalent to watchstanding engineering service.

CGC TAMAROA EWO 8 144 288

3000 hp AUX OFFICER 4 72 72

(2200 kW)

TOTAL 1134

The Tamaroa is under 4000 hp (3000 hp) so it can be used for up to 50% of the service required for an unlimited third's license. If more than 50% of the required service was on vessels under 4000 hp (3000 kW), a horsepower (power rating) limitation would be computed for the third's license.

Chapter Ten
The Future:
Staying Ahead of the Game

Throughout this book, I have been urging you to stay ahead of the game, ask questions, research jobs and certificates, and ensure all doors are open to you for employment by getting all the required endorsements and certificates by any means necessary. The only thing left for me to do is to emphasize this point. The mariner who keeps his or her finger on the pulse of our legal system, the unions, and shipping companies will know what new certificates or endorsements are going to be required and by what date. These certificates can be helpful in getting a job. If companies require certificates that only you have, guess who gets the job.

To stay on top of the latest maritime industry information, check in regularly with these Web sites:

▶ The National Archives Web Site (the *Federal Register*) www.nara.gov

This Web site is great to see what Congress is talking about each day regarding new laws and regulations. This site has a lot of information. The *Federal Register* is found on the tool bar at the left-hand side. Anytime you want to see what subjects the USCG or the Department of Homeland Security is proposing, check the *Federal Register.* This will really keep you informed on new policies affecting your MMD or license.

▶ The USCG Web Site: www.uscg.mil/stcw

This has been discussed too much already for you not to have the Web address emblazoned on your brain. Everything you need is on this site. Use it.

▶ The Code of Federal Regulations: www.gpoaccess.gov/cfr/index.html

This site lists all the CFRs. When you go to the site, click on "browse and/or search CFRs," and it will take you to the full menu. These are the rules governing our industry. Title 46, 33, and 49 of the CFRs apply to shipping.

▶ The U.S. Code: www.uscode.house.gov/usc.htm
This is another list of regulations, like the CFRs, that govern our industry.

▶ The International Maritime Organization: www.imo.org
This site is another great one to monitor for what is happening around the world of shipping. Any new requirements or any concerns the IMO might be looking at that could affect your license or MMD will be listed here. Check it periodically, like the *Federal Register.*

The last list is from the General Information for Merchant Mariner's Documents, Licenses, and STCW Certificates from the USCG Web site. Some of the pages are redundant, but some of them are new and good to keep on your list of references.

Information on the Internet

- USCG National Licensing Web site: www.uscg.mil/stcw/index.htm
- Code of Federal Regulations: www.access.gpo.gov/nara/cfr/index.html
- USCG Marine Safety: www.uscg.mil/hq/g-m/
- USCG National Maritime Center: www.uscg.mil/NMC
- National Driver Register (NDR): www.nhtsa.dot.gov/people/perform/driver/
- Vital Records Information (US): www.vitalrec.com/ 1 REV. 3/2004
- Social Security Administration: www.ssa.gov

Pursue any rumor. Validate it as fact or sea story. Talk to the professionals, Coast Guard, IMO, maritime schools, National Maritime Center, Veterans Administration, schools, and visit the Web site www.thenewhawsepipe.com. Find people who know what they are talking about.

Unfortunately, that usually includes the captain's and chief mates. Unless they are part-time instructors, they have limited experience with the new rules. They have already done everything and have no idea what it takes to get what you need. Just smile and nod your head because they will probably have some sort of answer anyway. Remember, validate. Check the Web sites, read the maritime magazines and newsletters.

Look for vessel security and port security to be at the top of the new-things-required list. I know some companies have already added Ship's Security Officer to the list of certificates needed. This book does not detail everything you need for every job, and I wish I could keep submitting revisions to keep everything up-to-date, but the truth is more certificates and classes will always be required, and it is your job is to keep informed.

New guidelines for sea service for some licenses also are coming down from the NMC regarding equivalencies for licenses. Just because you qualify for second mate unlimited doesn't mean you might qualify for 1,600 ton master anymore. Also, new information is coming out regarding medical physicals for USCG licenses. The physicals are going to be in greater detail for medical personnel to follow so that the physical is performed correctly and guidelines to follow granting medical waivers to merchant mariners.

Now that the United States has adopted STCW 95, the IMO continues to make new regulations for us to follow. Whether the other countries follow the regulations as closely as we do, I don't know. But I do know that the United States will always follow the regulations, and that means, by default, you will follow the regulations and jump through whatever hoops that come your way.

In the future, the Coast Guard will be centralizing its merchant mariner branches. This means that all the RECs will disappear, and one central bank will process all applications. The USCG is experimenting with it now and it will be up and running soon in West Virginia. The USCG is trying to minimize the differences between RECs throughout the country and regulate the procedures for testing and issuance of MMDs and licenses. Most things will be done electronically or by mail.

The good thing is, you should be able to get the same answers wherever you go. The bad news is, your local REC will be gone, and the relationships you built will not be as beneficial and things might take even longer. Talk to the REC to make sure you know when this is happening (projected in 2007/2008) and either get your paperwork in before. Keep this in mind while you are climbing up the hawsepipe. Do not forget to visit my Web site (www. thenewhawsepipe.com) and detail any experiences you had, good or bad, onto the page so we can help make this process and our jobs easier and better.

This book was written to straighten out the mess of regulations and make getting a merchant license a bit easier. I tried to write to the point, yet if you have any lingering confusion, please do not hesitate to ask me or somebody else who is familiar with the hawsepipe. This is very important information, and any confusion could make the climb more difficult, which would defeat the purpose of this book.

I hope you are now armed with easier and better tools to work with. If I missed anything or you pick up a new trick to this game, let me know on the Web site so others can benefit. Thanks for taking the time to read this, and good luck in your pursuits. Always keep your eye on the prize and never lose your motivation. This is more than possible. Do it!

Postscript
Being an Officer, Being a Leader

I got on a ship that had a new hawsepiper on his first job as a third mate. You should know now by reading this book that once you have the license or document in your hand, the job is yours. This particular individual was having a terrible time understanding the scope of his job and the mates were no help to him. They felt like it wasn't their job to carry this individual and teach him his duties. The other mates had gone to a maritime academy and didn't have the time or patience to teach a fellow mariner who was not grasping the new job at all.

The mates quickly circled around this hawsepiper and cut all ties to him, making him pay for any mistake and driving him extra hard to accomplish small tasks. This kind of cancer eventually spread to the unlicensed deck department and they started feeding on him. While on watch, the hawsepiper did not have the tools or experience needed to make solid decisions. His watch team capitalized on this and picked on him for not being able to make a competent decision. He yelled at his watch team to try to establish seniority, but it fell on deaf ears and made the crew like him less. He called the captain for problems that he should have been able to solve himself and the captain, mates, and deckhands told him so. He became more and more depressed as the crew distanced themselves from him. He was warned by the other mates that the captain was fed up with him and he should quit the job before he got fired. The hawsepiper did not know what to do. This was a really good paying job and he worked so hard to get his license and paid so much money for school that he needed to pay back. He had not committed any serious marine incidents and was a hard worker. He was learning as fast as he could, but it did not seem to help.

I reported onboard as the new second mate and fell upon this situation—a new hawsepiper that just got his license and his first job. I had just finished this manuscript and really did not know what to do. I did not want to make a huge production defending this third mate, distancing myself from the other mates before they even knew who I was, first impressions being a big deal in this industry. But I did not want this new hawsepiper to quit after working so hard to get his license and this job. This was the perfect candidate for me to help. This was also my first second mate's job and I had a lot of learning to do myself. So my dilemma was how far do you go to help someone else? Is there a limit to how much your fellow deck officers should help you? Is it their responsibility to teach you what they know? Some people do you a favor and merely hand you a pencil, then wipe the sweat from their brow and say, "So, do you think you can take it from here, because I am done."

I will never forget this situation. I pulled the hawsepiper aside and, without us knowing each other, I told him the worst thing he could do was quit and that he had not done anything that I had seen to warrant a captain firing him. He was a good worker and learning every day. I told him that I understood how hard it is being a hawsepiper on your first job. I told him I would help him as much as I could. I told him that he was a good officer.

I saw the appreciation in his eyes and he thanked me for the support and said he really did not like it onboard the ship, money be damned. I told him a job like this will not come around for a long time and to think about his decision and think about why he became an officer. He smiled and we parted ways.

The following morning he went to the captain's office and quit. The captain obliged and started processing his discharge. The hawsepiper came and told me that he could not take it anymore and was going to go back to being an AB to get more experience on another ship. This guy just wanted to get as far away from the ship as possible.

The worst part about this scenario was that the ship was great. The deck, engine, and stewarding department were awesome and the operation area was great, with plenty of time between ports and plenty of time in port for training and preparation. In fact, it was the perfect ship on which to learn.

I felt this was a terrible blow to hawsepipers. Once I got to know the deck officers and they knew who I was, I let them know what they just did to this guy. Unforgivable, but the tragic reality is this can happen at anytime to anyone.

When you step onboard, you must balance your lack of knowledge and inexperience in leadership with integrity and humbleness. You must let your shipmates know that you are eager to learn, and when you learn something, you do it. You must continue to progress upward. Think of yourself as an empty file cabinet. Once you put a file in it, do not make your shipmates explain it again. When you make a mistake, learn how to do it and do not make that mistake again.

Start by reading the standing orders of the vessel and the standard operating procedure for the company and the ship. These are the templates in which you follow. You will find that captains and mates place importance on different things. Some captains love drills, some love paperwork and forms, some love to get dirty on deck, some love navigation and shiphandling, and some don't know what they love so they love to yell. Most will be a matrix of all, but this is a wonderful time to learn their specialty. If you can cater to their operating procedure, your job will start to flow and you can ask more questions. The captains and mates do not expect you to know everything, but they expect you to know how and when to ask. After that, it is up to you to retain the knowledge. I guarantee that you can learn something from everybody. Comically, some of it has nothing to do with shipping, but nevertheless.

I believe in leading by example. You always hear, "Treat people the way you want to be treated." Never yell. Yelling only means you do not know your job. You will undoubtedly be a nervous wreck your first watch on your new job, with your new responsibility and every situation is different. Since you have no experience, remember the templates: your nav rules for traffic, standing orders for bridge watch, and procedures for drills. These are in place for you to reference before you get your sea sense, which will come. Let me tell you about my first time.

My very first mates job was on a tug and barge in Puget Sound, Seattle. It was a five-man crew and I had never sailed on my license before. The office called me and told me to show up at 2:00 a.m. at this certain dock and I would meet everybody there. The office told me that the crew knew I was new and to expect me on this run. I thanked him and tried to get some sleep before my first job as a merchant mariner.

After lying awake the entire time, I headed out for the dock. When I got there, some of the crew were loading ship's stores. I introduced myself and grabbed some bags on my way onboard.

When everybody showed up and we were ready to go, I followed the captain up to the bridge and asked the dumbest question ever. "I met everybody, but I haven't met the mate. Who is the mate?" He whirled around and stared at me.

"You are," he said.

"Oh, right, yeah, okay. No problem." I said. *Jesus, I can't believe I just said that.*

"No problem?" He raised an eyebrow.

"Yeah, no problem," I stammered. "I thought the company was going to give me the job as the deckhand first to ramp me up."

"You do have a license, right?" the captain asked.

"Yes, I do. Everything is fine. I can do the job. We are going to be fine." I knew I had to rely on my limited experience to get through this. I wasn't new and I could do this job, but I had to let this captain know that I was the mate and had no problem being the mate. I was the only other deck license, other than the captain.

We let the lines go, hooked up the barge, and paid out the tow until the captain was happy. We were cruising north for two days, towing an empty deck barge to load engine equipment and bring it back to Seattle. It was time for my watch, so I came up early to get the lowdown. The captain looked at me—he was a salty bastard—and asked, "So, you're from the Coast Guard, huh?"

I nodded my head and mumbled, "Yep."

He, obviously, was not from the Coast Guard and did not really like the fact that I was. He growled, "So, you got a knife?"

Damn. I had been so nervous I had forgotten my knife. It was sitting on my bed at home. I had put it there so I wouldn't forget it. Yeah, that worked. I swallowed my pride and said, "No, I don't. I forgot it."

"A knife can save your life out here," he yelled. "Don't ever step onboard without one, especially on my ship!"

He raised his left hand so it was right in front of my face. In the glow of the instrument panel, I could see that his thumb was missing.

"Things can happen out here. Make sure you got a knife," he said while staring at me.

I told him I would never forget it again, and I haven't to this day.

As I was grasping the electronics, which were all foreign to me, he said curtly "This is the wheel, this is the throttle, call if you get in trouble or have a question, and don't worry about what time it is. I'm going to bed. See ya."

I grabbed the helm and was too terrified to tell him I really didn't know what I was doing. I turned around and he was gone. It was me and, well, me. I took a quick situation analysis and tried to get my head around what was happening. We looked good so far. The weather was fine, tow looked good, the engine was rolling, and traffic was minimal. Okay, I can do this, I thought. I felt an excitement that this was the first bridge watch I was in charge of at twenty-one years old and I was truly a deck officer. That excitement was coupled with a sickly feeling that came from my nerves being on super-high alert. I was all over the bridge, trying to get a hold of everything while piloting through the traffic lanes of Puget Sound.

In the morning, a container ship was overtaking me and I was trying to get out of the way as much as possible. I knew my good Coast Guard training told me I should make contact via VHF radio, but I didn't want to bother them as they, well, they probably knew what they were doing. I grasped the radio, got all the information I thought I needed to confirm. I swallowed, and called the container ship a half mile off my starboard quarter on course such and such, speed such and such, this is the tug and barge so and so.

The ship came back and asked me what I wanted. I played it cool and asked them if they were headed to the Straits of Juan de Fuca like I was, and if I was far enough out of the way. The pilot came back and said, "Looks like you're going to Port Angeles."

Jesus. Was I supposed to be going to Port Angeles? I didn't think so. Where was I supposed to be going? Was it a river? After this lightning onslaught of questions in my head, I replied to the pilot onboard the container ship that I was just moving over for him and that I was really going to the Twin Rivers and thanked him for his reply. The Twin Rivers, that was where we were going. My God, how could I forget that?

As we turned west, I settled back into the bridge watch, another disaster averted, I thought. The container ship was on my beam and overtaking me just fine. Up ahead was a large marina off my port bow, and I could see a mast of a sailboat coming out of it behind the break wall exiting the marina. I stayed on my course and speed, and as we got closer the sailboat emerged from out of the break wall. I looked at it on the radar and it looked like it was going to cross right in front of me. I couldn't turn right because of the container ship and couldn't turn left because of the break wall to the marina. I grabbed the binoculars and took a good look at this sailboat that was quickly increasing my frustration. As I panned out, I scanned the hull of the craft and realized, no one was at the helm! I instantly radioed the sailboat…nothing. I radioed again…nothing. Oh, boy. Now, at this point, I had a good sweat going and was nervous as hell all over the bridge. Should I blow the horn? Would that piss off the container ship? Should I get the captain up? Will he be mad that I am in this situation? I realized I needed to do something and do it now. I grabbed the throttles and pulled back. As the engines changed pitch and the tug surged back and I surged forward, I deduced that I had made a terrible decision and I needed to get the rpms back up to where they were before anyone realized…

The footsteps up the ladder signaled the end of my career. Damn, and I was just getting started.

"What's going on?" the captain asked calmly.

"Well," I said, "I've got this guy on my port side and he is closing on me and I can't turn back into the lanes because of this container ship and I thought I should slow down, or blow the horn, or call somebody on the radio…ummm."

He was smiling. "They told me you were new."

"What?" I said.

"You're doing fine, but you should have called me like I said."

"I know, you're right. I'm sorry," I said. *Could I do anything right? I thought.*

"The speed change was enough to let the sailboat go by ahead of us, but let me show you some quick ways to tell if you are on a collision course with someone else."

After a two minute drill on visual and radar collision avoidance he quietly asked, "So, have you seen the barge?"

Jesus! The damn barge! I forgot all about it. I leapt out of the chair and ran out on the bridge to look behind me. The barge was completely sideways and gaining ground on us like a heat-seeking missile.

I took a moment to drop my shoulders, shake my head, and let the incompetence sink in. Wow, I never I knew I was this bad. As the captain grabbed the throttles and sped up to outrun and reposition the barge, he laughed. "Don't worry about it. You're going to be fine. This is your first job. Just make sure you keep learning. Go ahead and get something to eat and crash out for awhile. We'll wake you up for tie up."

I remember going down below in utter defeat. I mean, I thought I was good at this. I crawled into my rack and drifted off to a pathetic sleep.

After we tied up, loaded the barge, and headed back to Seattle, I headed up to the bridge and was ready for another go. I wasn't going to let this beat me.

"You ready to take it?" the captain asked.

"Yes I am," I said.

"Okay, here's what's happening," and the captain proceeded to give me all the information I needed for taking over the watch.

When he was through he said, "Call me when you have had enough and I will relieve you, and, please, call me if you are in doubt of anything at anytime."

"Okay, thanks," I said

I was determined to stand this watch to the best of my ability. I had my eye on everything. I referred to my training for any circumstances that came up, and felt the ease and confidence slowly come back to me. It felt good.

I knew the captain was testing me to see how much I could take or how quickly I would call him for something. I finally called him at 2:00 a.m. to wake him up and tell him that, at his leisure, he could come to the bridge for my relief. When he finally ascended to the bridge, the lights of downtown Seattle were staring at him. He said, "So you took it all the way in?"

I had stood the entire seven-hour watch by myself and let everybody sleep. Upon my relief, the captain said that I had done a good job and we were right on our ETA.

I thanked him and we talked about breaking the tow, tying up and all the other stuff that goes with it. I remember heading down to the deck and feeling like I made up for what I did on the last trip.

The point of this postscript is to say that everybody goes through growing pains more than once. It is how we learn. But the important thing is how you, as a professional mariner, deal with it. It is going to happen and it is not very fun. Learn from it and retain the knowledge. That is your experience. Throw yourself into situations that others would not. Never quit on yourself or the job. It is too important. And above all, admit what you do not know. Work on finding the answers and present them after you find them, because captains and mates know when you are making it up, so don't. Work as a member of a team and listen to your shipmates, all of them. Make your own decisions and give reasons why you made the decision. Being an officer, you should be an example of how to work as a team. Put forth the extra effort to do every job the right way and show people that they can count on you as a competent mariner.

It is all a balancing act of knowledge, attitude, experience, and personality. Each individual has their own matrix of these to become a respected, trusted, competent, and likeable team member of the ship's crew.

Index

About the Author

Leonard Lambert resides in Snohomish, Washington. He is a U.S. Coast Guard veteran who served aboard the USCGC *Polar Sea* and USCGC *Mallow* as a navigator (Quartermaster). He has worked as an able-bodied seaman for ChevronTexaco and government-contracted vessels (MSC) through the Seafarer's International Union. He has worked as a limited tonnage mate and master for a tug and barge, passenger vessels and coastal freighters in Puget Sound, including research vessels in the Gulf of Mexico. He has sailed as an unlimited second and third mate for government vessels through the IOMM&P, and Matson commercial container ships. He holds a second mate unlimited, 1,600 ton masters license and is working his way toward an unlimited masters license and an active membership to the IOMM&P. In his career he has been a working union member of SIU, Sailors' Union of the Pacific (SUP), Marine Engineers' Beneficial Association (MEBA), and IOMM&P. He received his BA from the University of Washington in communications and was one of the first hawsepipers in Seattle under the new STCW 95 rules. Leonard is a Coast Guard-approved and experienced instructor, who teaches for maritime schools in Puget Sound.